THE MAKING OF A MAN

Devotions for the Challenges
That Men Face in Family and Career

OTHER BOOKS BY RICHARD EXLEY

Abortion
Pro–Life by Conviction
Pro–Choice by Default

Blue–Collar Christianity

Perils of Power

The Rhythm of Life

The Painted Parable

The Other God —
Seeing God as He Really Is

Life's Bottom Line
Building Relationships That Last

When You Lose Someone You Love
Comfort for Those Who Grieve

THE MAKING OF A MAN

*Devotions for the Challenges
That Men Face in Family and Career*

by
Richard Exley

Tulsa, Oklahoma

6th Printing
Over 70,000 in Print

The Making of a Man — Devotions for the Challenges That Men Face in Family and Career
ISBN 1–56292–036–7
Copyright © 1993 by Richard Exley
P.O. Box 54744
Tulsa, Oklahoma 74155

Published by Honor Books
P. O. Box 55388
Tulsa, Oklahoma 74155

DEDICATION

This book is dedicated to Todd Allen Phillips, who is like a son to me, and to all the men whose friendships have enriched my life and enlarged my capacity for living. You know who you are, and I know that I will ever be in your debt.

CONTENTS

A MAN AND HIS TIME

"Once we begin wisely allotting time for reading and reflection, wondering and writing, we shall soon notice the reward. Life becomes less pressured. Christ, not the clock on the wall, becomes the center of our lives. Amazingly, we seem to accomplish more because our energy is not siphoned into pockets of useless worry. What a joy it is to make time our servant instead of our becoming enslaved to time."

— Susan Annette Muto

CHAPTER 1

HECTIC OR HOLY?

Today's man is in constant danger of becoming enslaved by the very things that were supposed to make his life more convenient. Notebook computers, fax machines, pagers, and cellular phones threaten to take him hostage. No matter where he goes, his work goes with him. In truth, his time (his life) is not his own.

Even if he could break free of the ever–encroaching demands of his career, his other responsibilities are enough to occupy his every waking moment, things like volunteer work at the church and civic duties, not to mention his family responsibilities. He needs to spend quality time with his children. He needs to be both physically and emotionally present for his wife. He needs to take care of the yard and service the cars. He needs to balance the checkbook. He needs...the list seems endless.

Somewhere in his hectic schedule he must find time to build lasting friendships, time to maintain a quality devotional life, time to read for personal and spiritual development, and time to exercise. No wonder he's tempted to throw up his hands in despair!

Is there a solution, a way out? I think so, but it won't be easy. Busyness is addictive and it's hard to regain command of our life once we've yielded it to the expectations of others. The key is control. Are we going to be governed by external pressures — the desires of others — or will we allow the internal witness of the Holy Spirit to set our agendas?

HECTIC OR HOLY?

ACTION STEPS:
■ Sit down with your wife and/or a trusted friend and ask for help in dividing your daily activities into four categories:

    1) Absolutely essential

    2) Important but not essential

    3) Helpful but not necessary

    4) Trivial[2]

■ Now eliminate everything in categories three and four.

Thought for the Day:
"We are too busy only because we want to be too busy. We could cut out a great deal of our activity and not seriously affect our productivity."[3]

— Richard Foster

"Let my body be a servant of my spirit and both my body and spirit be servants of Jesus, doing all things for your [God's] glory here."[4]

— Jeremy Taylor

Scripture for the Day:
"...All the days ordained for me were written in your book before one of them came to be."

— Psalm 139:16

CHAPTER 2

THE DIVINE ARBITRATOR

Busyness is a way of life for the nineties man, and frantic activity has become the norm. Initially, he is driven by the mistaken assumption that success will free him from his haunting self–doubt, but it does not. Unfortunately, by the time he comes to that realization he is usually a prisoner of his hectic lifestyle. An overcrowded calendar, the unending expectations of others, and emotional exhaustion are the dominating forces in his life.

Although his work isn't usually physically demanding, he often drags home hardly able to put one foot in front of the other. He's emotionally spent, his spirit is depleted. The constant pressure, the continual interaction with people, plus the multiplicity of roles required of him taxes his emotional energies. Add a touch of interpersonal conflict, and the drain increases dramatically.

"Within all of us," writes Richard Foster in *The Freedom of Simplicity*, "is a whole conglomerate of selves....Each one screams to protect his or her vested interests....No wonder we feel distracted and torn. No wonder we overcommit our schedules and live lives of frantic faithfulness."[1]

He goes on to suggest that a man cannot make peace with these competing demands until he surrenders control of his life to the "divine Arbitrator." Not self, nor others, but God must become the governing force in his life.

For me, this simply means living a God–centered life rather than a need–centered one. God's will, not the world's needs or even my own needs, becomes the focus of my life. As a result I experience an inner harmony which enables me to minister within my limits, both emotionally and physically, without feeling guilty. It's not easy, but it is the only way a conscientious man can find peace in our demanding world.

THE DIVINE ARBITRATOR

ACTION STEPS:

■ Make a list of all of the areas in which you serve as a volunteer. Now determine why you are serving in each area. Are you there by divine appointment, or out of a misguided sense of responsibility?

■ Set a reasonable time to resign from all volunteer positions except for those where you know God has placed you.

Thought for the Day:

"Toward them all [areas of human need] we feel kindly, but we are dismissed from active service in most of them. And we have an easy mind in the presence of desperately real needs which are not our direct responsibility. We cannot die on every cross, nor are we expected to."[2]

— Thomas R. Kelly

Scripture for the Day:

"So he, trembling and astonished, said, 'Lord, what do You want me to do?' And the Lord said to him, 'Arise and go into the city, and *you will be told what you must do.*'"

— Acts 9:6 NKJV

CHAPTER 3

THE RENEWING POWER OF SOLITUDE

inding time for yourself is a never–ending challenge. The world is constantly encroaching — an important meeting, your daughter's spring concert, special services at church, a new project. The list is endless. Again and again, you fall prey to the press of busyness, at least I do. And almost before I know it I find myself resenting the very things I once enjoyed.

Finally, out of necessity, I shut out the world for a few hours, sometimes even overnight. Then it comes back to me. I haven't been practicing "the rhythm of life."[1] I haven't made time for myself, time for solitude. Yet, even in the midst of that realization, I am severely tempted to turn on the radio or pick up the phone and call someone. Solitude has become a stranger, and I can hardly bring myself to seek it out.

With determined deliberateness, I do the things that have worked in the past. I brew a cup of coffee. I light the kerosene lamp in my study. I force myself to sit and be quiet. At first, half a hundred thoughts wrestle for my attention. Phone calls I need to make. Things I need to do tomorrow. Chores I should be doing around the house right now.

Resisting the temptation to tackle those tasks, I discipline myself to be still, and bit by bit I feel the tensions slip away. The noise of the world is pushed back for a little while. Even the discordant voices within grow quiet. And in the silence of God's presence I am renewed.

THE RENEWING POWER OF SOLITUDE

ACTION STEPS:
- Become aware of the little snatches of solitude that fill your day and take advantage of them.
- Experiment with devoting an entire evening to silence — no conversation, no radio or television, no telephone.
- Dedicate a time for solitude each day.

Thought for the Day:
"It is in this solitude that we discover that being is more important than having, and that we are worth more than the result of our efforts. In solitude we discover that our life is not a possession to be defended, but a gift to be shared."[2]

— Henri J. Nouwen

Scripture for the Day:
"But those who wait on the Lord shall renew their strength; they shall mount up with wings like eagles, they shall run and not be weary, they shall walk and not faint."

Isaiah 40:31 NKJV

CHAPTER 4

THE PLEASURE OF HIS PRESENCE

It was Sunday morning, early — about five–thirty — and the first hint of daylight was scrubbing the darkness from the sky. I was at my desk, preparing for the morning services, when I was suddenly overwhelmed with the most incredible sense of well being. My whole being was literally flooded with joy. At first I wasn't sure what caused it, or where it came from. Was it the pleasure that comes from being alone, without really being alone? My wife and daughter were asleep upstairs, and yet my sense of solitude was complete.

In the stillness of that moment I experienced a growing awareness of God's presence. It was as real as if He had assumed a physical form and was sitting in the room with me, comfortably close, but not intrusive. We were silent, but not separated by the silence. We were communicating, without words, like familiar friends, or a couple in love for whom words are unnecessary.

The silence was all encompassing, almost holy. There was no traffic on the streets, no noisy lawn mowers or blaring radios, no human voices either.

After a few minutes the press of time called me to the task of ministry, and I turned my attention to my sermon notes. I could almost see Him smile as I gave myself to the work I love. Yet, in that moment, I realized as never before that the work — the ministry — would be meaningless without the relationship.

Now, I've practiced the discipline of prayer long enough to know that that was a rare and special experience. Still, I cannot help but wonder how many holy moments I've missed simply because I let weariness, or busyness, keep me from the appointed hour. In truth, experience has taught me that God most often speaks to us out of silence, and if we truly want to experience His presence we must carve out a space for solitude in our busy lives.

THE PLEASURE OF HIS PRESENCE

ACTION STEPS:

- Remember a special spiritual experience. Where were you? What were you doing?
- Although you cannot recreate that experience, you can identify the spiritual disciplines that made you sensitive to God's presence. Disciplines like personal devotions at an appointed time and place, meditation, silence, and solitude.
- Now determine to practice those disciplines faithfully. Schedule them into your day the way you would any other important appointment.

Thought for the Day:

"The peak moments of ecstasy will be few and brief, but the memory of them abides, and something deep within us says that all the strivings of life are worthwhile because of them."[1]

— M. Basil Pennington

Scripture for the Day:

"When he [Jesus] was at the table with them, he took bread, gave thanks, broke it and began to give it to them. Then their eyes were opened and they recognized him, and he disappeared from their sight. They asked each other, 'Were not our hearts burning within us while he talked with us on the road and opened the Scriptures to us?'"

— Luke 24:30–32

CHAPTER 5

INVESTING IN THE ETERNAL

Are you investing your life in eternal things, or is it dominated by temporal concerns — your career, how much money you make, the kind of car you drive, where you live, etc.? All of these things are temporary, of little consequence in light of eternity. Unfortunately, we live in a culture that majors in the temporary, and if we are not careful we too will succumb to its fascination with the now. As a consequence, we risk reaching the end of our earthly sojourn only to discover that we have wasted our lives.

God, in His mercy, has built certain checkpoints into life which cause us to pause and reflect, to consider its true meaning. Things like births and baptisms, weddings and funerals, especially funerals. At such times we are brought face to face with the deep issues of life, and inevitably our thoughts turn to eternity.

Recently I had such an experience — when my Uncle Ernie died. He was not a great man as the world counts greatness. He was never the pastor of a large church, he never wrote a book, and he never made a name for himself. He was, however, a special man — a throwback to an earlier age when the measure of a man was determined by the quality of his character rather than the power of his personality.

If you don't look beneath the surface, his life seems rather insignificant, but on a deeper level it has eternal value. Only God knows how many men and women received Jesus Christ as their Savior as a result of Uncle Ernie's witness — and who can measure the value of a single soul?

Even in death his ministry lives on. He had a profound influence on my brother, Don, and his decision to become a missionary. Another nephew, Orville Stewart, is a pastor, and Uncle Ernie's ministry lives on in his work as well. Of course, anything I do, and whatever influence I have, is his also, for he gave me my start in the ministry and invited me to preach in every church where he was pastor.

As I think about him now, I realize as never before just how much of his life was spent on eternal things. In truth, he laid up for himself treasures in heaven. And his life causes me to pause and take stock of my own. I find myself asking, "Does my life have eternal value, or am I wasting my days chasing after the wind?"

Take a moment right now to examine your own life. Are you involved in Kingdom business or is your life dominated by the temporal? You don't have to be in "professional" ministry to be about the Master's business. It's an attitude, a way of relating to the people around you. When Jesus was asked who was the greatest in the Kingdom of God, He replied, "'The greatest among you will be your servant.'"[1]

ACTION STEPS:

- Contact the staff of your local rescue mission and ask if there is anything you can do to help them.
- Write to one of the missionaries your church supports and ask them how you can help them in their ministry.
- Do your good deeds in secret.

Thought for the Day:

"One hundred years from today your present income will be inconsequential. One hundred years from now it won't matter if you got that big break, took the trip to Europe, or finally traded up to a Mercedes....It will matter that you knew God. It will greatly matter, one hundred years from now, that you made a commitment to Jesus Christ."[2]

— David Shibley

Scripture for the Day:

"'...Provide purses for yourselves that will not wear out, a treasure in heaven that will not be exhausted, where no thief comes near and no moth destroys. For where your treasure is, there your heart will be also.'"

— Luke 12:33,34

A MAN AND HIS WORK

" **I** like to get paid for my work, but what fulfills me and makes me whole is the work, not the payment. I am involved in both, but if I am to be a whole person, I must know what is primary for me, and what is secondary. If I know that the quality and integrity of my work come first, then I am true to my profession both as writer and as a teacher. If money comes first, then I am corrupt — even if I never steal anything or accept a bribe. If I am unsure about which comes first, then I am morally confused and a divided person."[1]

— Max Lerner

CHAPTER 6

JOB SECURITY

G iven the current economic climate, it's not hard to see why a conscientious man could become obsessed with his work. Job security is a thing of the past. Major companies announce layoffs with disconcerting regularity. High–level executives are at risk just like the man on the assembly line. No job is secure. Tough economic times force companies to make hard decisions. Jobs must be eliminated, overhead must be cut, and that means greater competition for the jobs that are left.

Not infrequently a man is tempted to try and create his own job security. At least that is the way Mike explained his sixty–to seventy–hour work week. In order to insure his future with the company, he set out to become their most valuable employee. He was determined to exceed his superiors' expectations. He would work harder and be smarter than anyone else. And he succeeded, but at what cost?

He became a workaholic. He sacrificed everything — family, friends, church, and even his own personhood — for his job. It came first. When his wife talked with him about the situation, he became defensive, even angry. He was doing it for her and the children. It was only for a time. Once he was established, he would cut back.

But he didn't. His success was double–edged. With each promotion there came increased responsibilities. Now he had to work harder than ever just to keep up with the never–ending demands. The pressure was relentless.

What was really behind Mike's obsessive work ethic? Insecurity, and no little anxiety, to be sure, but I believe it goes even deeper than that. It was a spiritual problem, a misunderstanding about his relationship with the Father. Mike believed that taking care of his family was ultimately his responsibility. Jesus tells us that it is the Father's: "'...do not worry about your life, what you will eat; or about your body, what you will wear....For the pagan world runs after all such things, and your

Father knows that you need them. But seek his kingdom, and these things will be given to you as well.'"[2]

That doesn't mean that we don't have to work, but it does mean that our security is in God, not our work. Our primary responsibility, as obedient children, is to do the will of our Father in heaven. It is His responsibility to feed and clothe us and our family. It is He Who gives us our daily bread.

ACTION STEPS:

■ Make a list of the changes you would have to make in your daily life if you were to take seriously the admonition of Jesus to seek first the Kingdom of God.

■ Share your list with a friend and ask him to hold you accountable.

Thought for the Day:

"[The called man] sees himself as a steward....He's obedient rather than ambitious, committed rather than competitive. For him, nothing is more important than pleasing the One Who called him."[3]

— Richard Exley

Scripture for the Day:

"...the Lord was with Joseph and gave him success in whatever he did."

— Genesis 39:23

CHAPTER 7

CO–LABORERS WITH GOD

One day when Christopher Wren, the English architect, was directing the construction of St. Paul's Cathedral in London, he stopped to talk to one of the laborers at the building site. 'What do you do?' Wren inquired of the man. Not realizing that he was talking to the great architect, the man, who was a cement mixer, answered, 'Sir, can't you see? I'm building a great cathedral.'"[1]

I like that! Here was a man who was able to see past the limits of his job description to the grand scheme and to claim it as his own. He wasn't just mixing cement, he was building a beautiful cathedral. It was more than a job, more than a way of making a living. It was an opportunity to be part of something great, and he had sense enough to know it.

Such a perspective gives dignity to the most common labor, it makes us co–laborers with God. We are working with Him to feed, clothe, and shelter His human family. We share His dream for a world where poverty, disease, injustice, and unrighteousness have been obliterated. He is the eternal architect, we are just the cement mixers. Still, there's something grand about working with Him. It gives our life's work meaning and eternal value.

Remember, if you make the accumulation of wealth, or the pursuit of happiness, or any other personal benefit, the goal of your labors, you will find only futility. But, if you give yourself selflessly in service to God and others, God Himself will give you the desires of your heart. Fulfillment is not a goal. It is the consequence of a life lived in service to God and others!

ACTION STEPS:

- Make a conscious effort to see how your work contributes to God's provision for His human family. Be specific. List three or four of the ways you were able to identify.
- Make a commitment to do your work as unto the Lord.

Thought for the Day:

"It is not what a man does that determines whether his work is sacred or secular, it is why he does it."[2]

— A. W. Tozer

"The Bible knows nothing of a hierarchy of labor. No work is degrading. If it ought to be done, then it is good work."[3]

— Ben Patterson

Scripture for the Day:

"Whatever you do, work at it with all your heart, as working for the Lord, not for men, since you know that you will receive an inheritance from the Lord as a reward. It is the Lord Christ you are serving."

— Colossians 3:23,24

CHAPTER 8

TRUSTING GOD WITH YOUR CAREER

Ben was a young executive with a bright future. He was talented and hard working, and it seemed only a matter of time until his efforts would be rewarded with a corner office. Still, the pressures of corporate life were taking their toll. He was constantly required to choose between his family and his work, between his church and his career. Much of the pressure he felt came from the unspoken expectations of his superiors. He was expected to excel. They were counting on him.

When he came to see me, he was trying to sort it all out. As a sincere Christian he wanted to do what was right, yet he wanted to succeed in his career too. How, he wanted to know, could he balance all of the demands being placed on him? How could he be the kind of husband and father God expected him to be without taking time and energy away from his job? How could he remain active in his church without sacrificing his career? To his way of thinking, it was a time problem. There just didn't seem to be enough hours in a day.

After listening to him pour out his frustrations, I inquired, "Can you trust God with your career?"

"What do you mean?" he asked, puzzled.

"It sounds to me like you are trusting in your own strength, the long hours you work, the number of calls you make, things like that."

When he nodded I continued, "What we are really talking about is a matter of trust. Do you really believe that God can take care of your career?

"The way I read the Scriptures, that means a man would put God first, his family second, and his job third. That doesn't mean he would be careless or indifferent about his work, but only that he would not allow work to rob him of the time and energy that belong to God and his family. When a man honors God with the firstfruits of his time and energy, he is demonstrating his confidence in Him. He is trusting God to make his labors fruitful."

Ben thought about that for a few minutes, and then we prayed together, committing ourselves to seek first the Kingdom of God. It was a commitment he would have to renew day by day, and it wasn't always easy. Still, as the weeks passed he discovered that his production was up, even though the number of hours he worked was down. God honored his obedience.

ACTION STEPS:

- Make a conscious decision to trust God with your career.
- On your calendar block off time for God and your family, and refuse to allow work to intrude on it.

Thought for the Day:

"No matter what our occupations are — musician, garbage collector, football coach — when we come to Christ we all become Christian workers first, musicians, garbage collectors or football coaches, second. Whatever our 'callings,' we are preeminently called to serve Christ in and through our work."[1]

— Ben Patterson

Scripture for the Day:

"Do you see a man skilled in his work?
He will serve before kings;
he will not serve before obscure
men."

— Proverbs 22:29

CHAPTER 9

CALLED TO SERVE

A young woman, who worked as a maid, was converted to Jesus Christ and applied for membership in the church where Charles Spurgeon was pastor. As was the custom in that church, she was required to appear before the membership committee. In the course of the interview, Spurgeon asked her if there was any evidence that she had truly repented of her sins. Without hesitating she replied, "Now I don't sweep the dirt under the rugs in the house where I am employed." Spurgeon then turned to the others sitting on the committee and said, "It is enough. We will receive her."[1]

Her response, I believe, illustrates the difference Christ makes in the way we understand ourselves and our work. Without Christ we are self–centered and our work is primarily a way of meeting our own needs. In Christ we are God–centered and others–centered. As a consequence, our work becomes a way of honoring Christ through our service to others, especially our employer and the customers he serves.

To be God's servant in the work place is not easy. Not infrequently the work place is filled with tension and office politics, not to mention petty jealousies and personality conflicts. It's often a dog–eat–dog environment as co–workers are encouraged to compete against each other. It's every man for himself, and may the "best" man win.

The Bible calls us to be a different kind of people: "Do nothing out of selfish ambition or vain conceit, but in humility consider others better than yourselves. Each of you should look not only to your own interests, but also to the interests of others."[2]

ACTION STEPS:

■ Look for ways in which you can affirm and encourage your co–workers. If possible, take the time to put it in the form of a memo and send a copy to their supervisor.

■ Look for ways to go beyond the call of duty in the performance of your responsibilities, especially if it makes your supervisor or co–workers look good.

Thought for the Day:

"One corporate president told me he looked for three qualities in a person when he considered him or her for employment: attitude, enthusiasm, and zest for life. He said he can nurture the skills, but a person's attitude is a matter of choice. And attitude determines a person's potential to a company."[3]

— Dwain Jones

Scripture for the Day:

"Do not withhold good from those who
        deserve it,
    when it is in your power to act.
Do not say to your neighbor,
    'Come back later; I'll give it
        tomorrow' —
    when you now have it with you."

— Proverbs 3:27,28

CHAPTER 10

CELEBRATE YOUR ACHIEVEMENTS

On the day that Gov. Bill Clinton of Arkansas was nominated as the Democrat Party's candidate for the office of president of the United States, he told a news commentator, "God doesn't give you many days like this."

Regardless of how you feel about Bill Clinton, you have to appreciate the fact that he had the good sense to celebrate that moment. Far too often we succumb to the temptation to overlook our achievements, to miss those moments, simply because we haven't yet reached our ultimate goal.

In fact, I can imagine some campaign strategist raining on his parade. "Bill, this is just another small step on the long journey to the White House. There will be time enough to celebrate later. Right now we've got work to do."

That's the kind of thing coaches tell their teams after they win the first round of the play–offs. Upon first hearing it sounds good, but upon closer examination it contains a tragic flaw. It replaces appreciation with ambition and thus robs us of the joy of our achievement. In the long term, it means that while we may achieve success we will probably never experience fulfillment.

"In a world where not everyone will do great deeds or achieve great success," writes Harold Kushner, "God has given us the capacity to find greatness in the everyday....The good life, the truly human life, is based not on a few great moments but on many, many little ones. It asks of us that we relax in our quest long enough to let those moments accumulate and add up to something."[1]

CELEBRATE YOUR ACHIEVEMENTS

ACTION STEPS:

■ Make a list of your achievements, things like: graduating from high school, landing your first job, getting married, becoming a parent, closing that big sale, or getting a promotion.

Now plan a special evening to savor the joy of those moments with your family or friends.

■ Since all good things come from God, determine to take time out each day to thank Him for His blessings in your life.

Thought for the Day:

"In the world to come, each of us will be called to account for all the good things God put on earth, which we refused to enjoy."

— Talmud

Scripture for the Day:

"This is the day the Lord has made;
let us rejoice and be glad in it."

— Psalm 118:24

CHAPTER 11

DON'T BE AFRAID TO FAIL

When we see successful people, we often assume that they "got all the breaks," that they were always in the right place at the right time, that they've never failed, never been rejected. If the truth were known, very few people accomplish anything worthwhile the first time they attempt it. In fact, even the most successful people generally have a checkerboard career of both success and failure.

For years Alexander Graham Bell was a failure, at least he suffered one humiliating setback after another. He spent much of his life being laughed at and ridiculed as he crisscrossed New England trying to raise venture capital for the production of his invention — the telephone. Today nobody laughs at Bell. But he had to overcome failure in order to succeed.

When Walt Disney went around Hollywood with his little "Steamboat Willie" cartoon idea, he was bankrupt and by all normal standards a failure. Johnny Carson's first effort at his own network show was a terrible flop and for years he was a forgotten man. Today he is the standard by which all T.V. personalities are judged.

Like many others, all these people experienced painful, and sometimes humiliating, failure, but they refused to give up. Instead of allowing failure to defeat them, they stubbornly pursued their dreams and eventually attained them.

I once heard a noted psychiatrist say that the two saddest words in the human vocabulary are "if only." He went on to explain that many people are trapped in their failures and spend a lifetime saying "if only": If only I had tried harder. If only I had been a better parent. If only I hadn't been unfaithful. If only....

He suggested that we substitute the words "next time": Next time I will use better judgment. Next time I will be a better parent, a better husband. Next time I will try harder.

DON'T BE AFRAID TO FAIL

"If only" focuses on past failures and sentences us to a lifetime of regret. "Next time" turns our attention to the future and inspires us to try again.

ACTION STEPS:

■ If you have experienced a painful failure, examine it and learn from it. Make a list of the mistakes you made and determine what you will do differently next time. Now make a mental note of the lessons you learned — but forget about the failure.

■ Dare to dream again. Ask God to inspire you to attempt great things.

Thought for the Day

"...failing doesn't make [you] a failure. Giving up, accepting [your] failure, refusing to try again, does!"[1]

— Richard Exley

Scripture for the Day:

"...though a righteous man falls seven
times, he rises again...."

— Proverbs 24:16

A MAN AND HIS WIFE

"**W**inston Churchill once attended a formal banquet in London, where the dignitaries were asked the question, 'If you could not be who you are, who would you like to be?' Naturally everyone was curious as to what Churchill, who was seated next to his beloved Clemmie, would say. After all, Churchill could not be expected to say Julius Caesar or Napoleon. When it finally came Churchill's turn, the old man, the last respondent to the question, rose and gave his answer. 'If I could not be who I am, I would most like to be' — and here he paused to take his wife's hand — 'Lady Churchill's second husband.'"[1]

— James Humes

CHAPTER 12

THE HIGH COST OF COMMITMENT

In March 1990, Dr. Robertson McQuilkin announced his resignation as president of Columbia Bible College in order to care for his beloved wife, Muriel, who was suffering from the advanced stages of Alzheimer's disease. In his resignation letter he wrote:

"My dear wife, Muriel, has been in failing mental health for about eight years. So far I have been able to carry both her ever–growing needs and my leadership responsibilities at CBC. But recently it has become apparent that Muriel is contented most of the time she is with me and almost none of the time I am away from her. It is not just 'discontent.' She is filled with fear —even terror — that she has lost me and always goes in search of me when I leave home. Then she may be full of anger when she cannot get to me. So it is clear to me that she needs me now, full–time.

"Perhaps it would help you to understand if I shared with you what I shared at the time of the announcement of my resignation in chapel. The decision was made, in a way, 42 years ago when I promised to care for Muriel 'in sickness and in health...till death do us part.' So, as I told the students and faculty, as a man of my word, integrity has something to do with it. But so does fairness. She has cared for me fully and sacrificially all these years; if I cared for her for the next 40 years I would not be out of debt. Duty, however, can be grim and stoic. But there is more; I love Muriel. She is a delight to me — her childlike dependence and confidence in me, her warm love, occasional flashes of that wit I used to relish so, her happy spirit and tough resilience in the face of her continual distressing frustration. I do not have to care for her, I get to! It is a high honor to care for so wonderful a person."[2]

As a man and a husband, I am deeply moved when I read that. Intuitively I realize that's the stuff real marriages are made of — commitment and integrity, for better or for worse. Yet it would be a

THE HIGH COST OF COMMITMENT

mistake for us to assume that Dr. McQuilkin's decision was an isolated choice, independent of the hundreds of lesser choices that went into their forty–two years of marriage. In truth, a decision of that magnitude is almost always the culmination of a lifelong series of smaller, daily decisions. And, as such, it challenges every man to examine the choices he makes each day and the way he relates to his wife.

ACTION STEPS:
■ Ask yourself: Does my marriage get the leftovers and scraps from my busy day, or do I give it priority time and energy?
■ Make a list of the "little" ways in which you regularly lay down your life for your wife. Things like giving up Monday night football to spend the evening with her, or giving up a Saturday afternoon golf game to watch the children so she can go shopping with a friend.
■ Based on your daily decisions do you think you could give up your career in order to care for your wife if she became an invalid?

Thought for the Day:
"...nothing is easier than saying words.
Nothing is harder than living them, day after day.
What you promise today must be renewed and redecided tomorrow and each day that stretches out before you."[3]

— Arthur Gordon

Scripture for the Day:
"Husbands, love your wives, just as Christ loved the church and gave himself up for her to make her holy, cleansing her by the washing with water through the word, and to present her to himself as a radiant church, without stain or wrinkle or any other blemish, but holy and blameless."

— Ephesians 5:25–27

CHAPTER 13

I LOVE YOU

oo many men, I'm afraid, are like the elderly Vermont man who was reared to believe that silence was eternally golden. One night he and his wife were rocking silently, side by side, when he muttered painfully, "Sometimes, Maudy, I love you so much it's almost more than I can do not to tell you."[1]

That would be funny if it weren't so tragic. And it's not as far-fetched as you might think. You would be absolutely amazed at the number of men who find it nearly impossible to say, "I love you." Then again, maybe you wouldn't. At least, not if you are one of those men who have been described as the strong, silent type.

I once counseled with a couple who were at odds over this very issue. The wife was hurting. She was feeling lonely and insecure. Distinctly I remember her saying to her husband, "You haven't told me you love me since the night you proposed."

Disgruntled, he replied, "Well, nothing's changed, and when it does you'll be the first to know."

Unfortunately, his insensitive reply did little to warm their rapidly cooling relationship.

Another equally silent type told his wife, "Of course I love you. I make a good living for you and the kids, don't I?"

Indeed he did, and his wife was grateful, but she needed more than his paycheck to feel loved. Deeds may suffice for most men, but women need words as well as deeds to assure them that they are loved and appreciated.

According to Dr. James Dobson, "...genuine love is a fragile flower. It must be maintained and protected if it is to survive. Love can perish...when there is no time for romantic activity...when a man and his wife forget how to talk to each other."[2]

ACTION STEPS:

■ Determine right now that at least once a day you are going to tell your wife that you love her. If possible, stop what you are doing right now and tell her, even if you have to telephone her.

■ Ask God to help you become more complimentary. Determine that you will compliment your wife on her appearance, her homemaking skills, her hospitality, etc. Be creative. Find other equally valid ways to affirm her value as a person.

■ As a special gesture, sit down and write her a love letter.

Thought for the Day:

"Speaking and doing are two sides of a single coin. Only the word clarifies beyond doubt the great mystery of love's motivation behind the acts that make life smooth. Only the word carries the constant reminder in the doldrums of mundane activity; only the word sings in the ear and repeats itself in the memory."[3]

— Dorothy T. Samuel

Scripture for the Day:

"If a man has recently married, he must not be sent to war or have any other duty laid on him. For one year he is to be free to stay at home and bring happiness to the wife he has married."

— Deuteronomy 24:5

CHAPTER 14

KEEPING ROMANCE IN YOUR MARRIAGE

I can almost see you grimacing as you read the title of this chapter. "Romance," you mutter, "is for teenagers." I couldn't agree with you more, that is, if all we mean by romance is moonlight and music. But if we are talking about a relationship in which two individuals are committed to one another for life, then that's another matter all together. And if their relationship is to become all that God wants it to be, they will have to show mutual respect, share deep feelings, cultivate kindness, express affection, and cherish one another. Now that's real romance!

Unfortunately, a marriage like that is rare indeed. More often than not, it is just a forgotten dream, a newlywed hope, soon crushed beneath the demands of living. Studies indicate that only about 10 percent of all marriages ever reach their relational potential, while the rest struggle along in mediocrity or end in divorce.

Think of it! Marriage, which was created by God to end the loneliness of human beings, is often the loneliest place of all. Couples live in the same house, share the same bed, parent the same children, even make "love," yet they never really touch each other. They are together, but alone.

But it doesn't have to be that way. God still intends for marriage to be a special relationship, one in which two people truly become one with each other, experience the deepest intimacy, and discover the most complete fulfillment of which they are capable.

It doesn't just happen, though. In reality, marriage is both a gift and a discipline. God gives us each other and the tools for cultivating our blessed oneness, but it is up to us to work the soil of our relationship all the days of our lives. As men, our first order of business is to recognize the divinely designed differences between men and women.

For instance, we men tend to feel loved when our wives treat us with respect, are sensitive to our personal needs, and care for our home and children.

Our wives, on the other hand, need kind words, a touch of romance, as well as tenderness and appreciation. In addition, they often want and need a public demonstration of our love. Nothing inappropriate, of course, just some small gesture of affection — holding her hand, touching her shoulder for just a moment, taking her arm as we cross the street. Little things which say to her, and to the world, "I love this woman. I'm glad she's my wife."

Which brings us to another point — in marriage, little things mean a lot, especially to a woman. In fact, they can make the difference between a mediocre marriage and a really good one, one in which romance is alive and well. It's usually not the expensive gifts or the foreign vacations that determine the quality of a marital relationship, but the little things. A love note or an "unbirthday" card for her. A kind word, help with the children, a listening ear, the feeling that we really care. This is the stuff of which real marriages are made!

ACTION STEPS:

■ Make a list of some of the special moments you have shared with your wife. Things like the birth of your children, a special trip, holiday memories, an adversity shared and overcome.

■ Now write your wife a series of love notes reminiscing about those special memories.

Thought for the Day:

"Maintaining a healthy marriage does not eliminate temptation, but it does minimize its impact. When my deepest spiritual and emotional needs are met in relationship with God and my wife, I can respond as a whole person to those who seek my counsel and support. Since my needs are being fulfilled in appropriate ways, I will not need to use ministry situations as a means for establishing my value as a person. I may still be tempted, but now I can respond out of wholeness rather than need."[1]

— Richard Exley

Scripture for the Day:

"May your fountain be blessed,
    and may you rejoice in the wife of your youth.
A loving doe, a graceful deer —
    may her breasts satisfy you always,
    may you ever be captivated by her love."

— Proverbs 5:18,19

CHAPTER 15

INTIMACY IS MORE THAN SEX

If you've been married for any length of time, you've probably already discovered that there are some real differences between the way you perceive life and the way your wife does. Your relationship is not unique. While differences may vary from couple to couple, the truth is that men experience life through a different set of grids than women. Nowhere are these differences more pronounced than in the areas of sex and intimacy.

Men tend to think of intimacy in sexual terms, while most women think of it in relational or romantic terms. Hence the potential for a painful misunderstanding. As one wife put it, "I wish that he could understand that each time I kiss him or hug him or caress him...[it] is not an invitation to the bedroom."

A man's inability to understand his wife's need for nonsexual affection often leads to heated arguments and emotional distancing. Although his wife longs for his caresses, she begins rejecting his attempts at affection lest he think she is encouraging a sexual encounter when all she wants is tenderness and closeness. Not infrequently he interprets her actions as a personal rejection, and the gap between them widens.

"If I had to make a permanent choice between sex and affection," a thirty–six–year old wife explained, "I would choose affection. I love sex and have a need for it, but not when I am worn to a frazzle by my four kids, the car pool, and housework. My need for affection is greater during times of stress and my desire for sex is diminished. My husband thinks sex is affection. When I try to explain the difference, he does not understand."

In truth, marital intimacy is both relational and sexual. As we become emotionally intimate with our spouse, sex takes on a whole new dimension — not only the merging of our flesh but the touching of our souls. The Bible describes this act of love between a husband and a wife as a "knowing": "And Adam knew Eve his wife; and she conceived...."[1]

This oneness is called bonding, or what Dr. Desmond Morris identifies as "...the emotional covenant that links a man and woman together for life....the specialness which sets those two lovers apart from every other person on the face of the earth."[2]

This blessed oneness is embryonic to begin with. That is, it is true in the spirit of our relationship, but not necessarily in the reality of our day–to–day lives. We do not suddenly become one simply because a minister pronounces

INTIMACY IS MORE THAN SEX

us husband and wife. It's a process. It takes time and commitment, not to mention love, understanding, and hard work.

Although this may be the most demanding endeavor you've ever attempted, I can assure you that it is well worth the effort. Once your wife feels understood by you, once she is secure in the nonsexual intimacy of your emotional bonding, she will become more receptive to your sexual overtures. An added benefit is the closeness, the openness, in your relationship, which may well meet a need you didn't even realize you had.

ACTION STEPS:
■ Make a special effort to be sensitive to the needs of your wife. Be aware of her schedule and the kind of demands being made upon her. Shower her with nonsexual affection, especially during times of stress.

■ Emotional closeness is very important to a woman. It makes her feel loved, understood, and secure. To facilitate this kind of closeness you will need to practice reflective listening. That is, you must learn to non–judgmentally reflect her feelings back to her. Although you may want to "fix" her feelings, you must resist that temptation. She doesn't want you to fix anything; she just wants you to understand.

■ Make a special effort to get in touch with your own feelings and then share them with your wife. You may be surprised at how "intimate" that feels.

Thought for the Day:
"Sex is used differently by men and women in a love relationship. Many women view sharing as being close and men view being close as something sexual. Women view sex as one way of being close and too many men view it as the only way to be close. For women, tenderness, touching, talking, and sex go together. For some men, sex is sufficient, especially if they do not know how to relate in other forms of intimacy."[3]

— H. Norman Wright

Scripture for the Day:
"The Lord God said, 'It is not good for the man to be alone. I will make a helper suitable for him.' So the Lord God caused the man to fall into a deep sleep; and while he was sleeping, he took one of the man's ribs and closed up the place with flesh. Then the Lord God made a woman from the rib he had taken out of the man, and he brought her to the man.

"The man said, 'This is now bone of my bones and flesh of my flesh; she shall be called "woman," for she was taken out of man.'

"For this reason a man will leave his father and mother and be united to his wife, and they will become one flesh.

"The man and his wife were both naked, and they felt no shame."

Genesis 2:18,21–25

CHAPTER 16

LOVE AND ANGER

marital quarrels are inevitable and every couple will disagree sooner or later, even committed Christians. While conflict is uncomfortable, it is not necessarily bad. In fact, a "fair" fight can actually contribute to the quality of your marriage. If you can learn to use your quarrels to resolve your differences, then anger can be constructive rather than destructive. With that thought in mind, let me give you five rules for productive conflict resolution.

Rule # 1: Use "I" messages rather than "you" messages. An "I" message focuses on the speaker rather than the person being spoken to. For example, "You make me so mad" is a "you" message, and it attacks the person being addressed. On the other hand, "I feel angry when you do that," is an "I" message, and it focuses on the speaker, making him responsible for his feelings. By using "I" messages, you give your wife a chance to evaluate what you are saying without feeling the need to defend herself.

Rule # 2: Practice reflective listening. Reflective listening is demanding under the best of conditions, and it can seem almost impossible when you are in the heat of an argument. But if you can force yourself to listen carefully before you speak, you will discover that the rewards are well worth the effort.

In the heat of an argument we are almost always tempted to defend ourselves, or at least to explain ourselves. Reflective listening forces us to control that defensive instinct. Instead of defending yourself, you might say: "It sounds like you feel hurt and angry when I make a major decision without consulting you."

A statement like that does at least two things. First, it lets her know that you hear what she is saying and that her thoughts and feelings are important. Second, it allows her to clarify and expand until you truly understand why she feels the way she does. Practice reflective listening consistently and you will not only grow in your understanding of each other, but you will resolve some thorny issues as well.

Rule # 3: Stick to the issue! Many couples never resolve anything when they fight because they can't stick to the issue. Let me illustrate: Perhaps you thoughtlessly discard your clothes all over the house. How does that make your wife feel? Angry? Unappreciated? Hurt?

There's a number of ways she can handle that situation. She can withdraw and punish you with silence. She can attack you by telling you what an insensitive slob you are. She can nag you with sarcastic remarks, "Thanks for helping me keep the house picked up. I've only worked on it all day." Or she can use an "I" message. Something like, "I feel unappreciated when you leave your clothes all over the house, especially after I've spent all day cleaning."

If you are like a lot of husbands, you are probably more interested in winning the fight than in solving the problem. In that case, you will probably change the subject and mount an attack. "When you clean out your sewing room you can talk to me about my dirty socks, but until then I don't want to hear it."

With those words the battle lines are drawn and the war is on. Now it's a full–fledged argument, and not the kind that solves anything either. This destructive nonsense will likely continue until bedtime and then you will probably go to bed, back to back, with anger heavy between you.

The problem here is a common one — an inability or an unwillingness to stick to the issue. In counseling I often address this problem by asking the couple to sit side by side rather than facing each other. Next I ask them to imagine that the issue is on the other side of the table facing them. Then I say, "That's your enemy. You are on the same side! Now let's find a solution."

Let me illustrate. My wife is something of a perfectionist and she tends to focus on flaws when evaluating anything. That's not all bad, but needless to say, for years it was an ongoing source of frustration in our marriage. Don't misunderstand me; Brenda isn't critical. But if I asked her opinion, she inevitably responded in the negative, which frustrated me to no end.

Finally, she suggested that instead of asking, "How do you like this?" or, "What do you think?" that I ask, "What do you like about this?" As a result she has become much more positive and we have "solved" one of the hangnails which haunted our marriage.

Why don't you try something like that the next time you find yourself caught in the same old argument? Ask yourself: How can I help my wife solve this? or even, How can she help me solve this? Instead of attacking each other, why not join forces and attack the issue?

Rule # 4: Don't hit below the belt. If you have been married for any length of time, you know where your spouse is vulnerable, you know how to hurt her, and she knows how to hurt you. I'm thinking of a man whose first wife left him for another man. When he asked her to come back, she laughed and ridiculed him. When he demanded an explanation, she said, "You're a lousy lover. You've never once satisfied me." Needless to say, he was devastated.

A couple of years passed and he remarried. During a tender moment he shared that painful secret with his new wife. Some months later in the heat of battle she used it against him. "It's not hard to see why your first wife took a lover," she said cruelly.

That's what I mean by hitting below the belt. She won the argument, but the marriage was badly wounded.

Rule # 5: Don't go to bed mad. Unresolved anger can turn into bitterness almost overnight. That's why Paul said, "...let not the sun go down upon your wrath."[1] Nothing is more important than ending the conflict and renewing the relationship before calling it a day.

When forgiveness is freely given, and fully received, a miracle takes place — anger dies; hurt and bitterness are replaced with love. Tenderness takes up residence where hostility once reigned. Communication is restored and old hurts are replaced by bright hopes. Once again marriage is a safe place in a demanding world.

ACTION STEPS:
- Memorize the five steps to productive conflict resolution:
  1) Don't attack. Use "I" messages rather than "you" messages.
  2) Practice reflective listening.
  3) Stick to the issue.
  4) Don't hit below the belt.
  5) Don't go to bed mad.

LOVE AND ANGER

■ Ask yourself: In my marital quarrels am I a problem—solver or a warrior? Warriors focus on winning the argument, while problem—solvers concentrate on resolving the issue. Warriors look for a win/lose solution, while problem—solvers look for win/win solutions.

Thought for the Day:

"There is an old story about a sheepherder in Wyoming who would observe the behavior of wild animals during the winter. Packs of wolves, for example, would sweep into the valley and attack the bands of wild horses. The horses would form a circle with their heads at the center of the circle and kick out at the wolves, driving them away. Then the sheepherder saw the wolves attack a band of wild jackasses. The animals also formed a circle, but they formed it with their heads out toward the wolves. When they began to kick, they ended up kicking one another.

"People have a choice between being as smart as a wild horse or as stupid as a wild jackass. They can kick the problem or they can kick one another."²

— H. Norman Wright

Scripture for the Day:

"Husbands, in the same way be considerate as you live with your wives, and treat them with respect as the weaker partner and as heirs with you of the gracious gift of life, so that nothing will hinder your prayers. Finally, all of you, live in harmony with one another; be sympathetic, love as brothers, be compassionate and humble. Do not repay evil with evil or insult with insult, but with blessing, because to this you were called so that you may inherit a blessing."

— 1 Peter 3:7-9

CHAPTER 17

A LOVING LEADER

I t is not easy for today's man to fulfill his responsibilities as a husband and a father. The complexity of modern life and the increasing confusion about gender roles have left many men in limbo. Fifty years ago life was simpler. The roles for men and women were more clearly defined and better understood. Now all of that has changed. The aggressive feminist movement has not only called into question the traditional role of women, but the masculine role as well.

In my grandfather's day, or even in my father's day, the man made the living, and the woman made the home. After putting in a hard day on the job, a man was free to spend a quiet evening with his feet propped up. Most of the household chores and child–rearing responsibilities fell to the woman. Today things are different. Often both the husband and wife are employed outside the home. They share household duties and parenting responsibilities. In addition, today's husband and father is expected to be a sensitive lover, an understanding listener, a child psychologist, and the spiritual head of the home, as well as the principal breadwinner. That's a challenging role for the best of men, and an overwhelming one for many.

I'm not suggesting, not even for a moment, that the old way was better. In fact, I will be the first to admit that the tyrannical role many husbands and fathers have played for generations needed to be rewritten, but we must not throw out the baby with the bath water. In our efforts to provide women with the respect they deserve, we must not abandon the biblical roles for husbands and wives. Social customs may change, but the Word of God is eternal and must always be the basis for the roles of both men and women.

The Scriptures have some rather straightforward instructions for those of us who are husbands and fathers. In Ephesians chapter five, we are charged with the responsibility for maintaining the marital relationship. "For the husband is the head of the wife as Christ is the head of the church....Now as the church submits to Christ, so also wives should submit to their husbands in everything. Husbands, love your wives, just as Christ loved the church and gave himself up for her."[1]

From this passage it should be clear that our role as a husband is to provide both leadership and love. Many men get into trouble right here because they try to provide one without the other, or because they become overbalanced in one or the other. Assertive men often tend to lead without loving, but a more common problem in the nineties is men who love but don't lead. According to Jack Mayhall, "Leadership without love usually results in tyranny; but in marriage, love without leadership leads to unstable fanciful romanticism."[2]

But Spirit–directed, responsible leadership, richly seasoned with unselfish love, produces healthy marriages in which both spouses, as well as the children, are secure in their roles. In addition, such families are the foundation of society and our hope for the future.

ACTION STEPS:

■ It is impossible to be the kind of husband and father God expects you to be apart from the enablement of His Holy Spirit, but with God's help you can do all things. Why not bow your head right now and ask God to empower you to fulfill your responsibilities as the loving leader in your home. Make this prayer a part of your daily life.

■ Sit quietly for a few minutes and meditate on ways in which you can minister to your wife and children. Jot down the thoughts and ideas that come to you. Remember, this is often the way God speaks to us.

■ Now set a time when you will implement the insights God has given you. We must be "doers" of the word God speaks to us, not just "hearers."

Thought for the Day

"Unlike those partners today who try to duplicate one another's function in all but sex, and who value independence over unity, my parents seemed to feel dependency on each other was desirable. They achieved their individuality by assuming different roles in their marriage — clear–cut, well–defined responsibilities for which each was needed and on which neither intruded....Together they reinforced their shared dreams of education and travel and useful work for themselves and their children....Could every generation before now have been wrong?"[3]

— Joyce Caloney

Scripture for the Day:

"In this same way, husbands ought to love their wives as their own bodies. He who loves his wife loves himself. After all, no one ever hated his own body, but he feeds and cares for it, just as Christ does the church."

— Ephesians 5:28,29

CHAPTER 18

SIX PRINCIPLES OF A LOVING LEADER

According to the Scriptures, the roles of men and women in marriage are equal in value but different in function. It's critically important for a man to understand this or he may be tempted to "lord" it over his wife. He is the head of his home, but that does not make him more important than his wife, just more responsible before God.

According to Ephesians 5, he is charged with the responsibility of providing both love and leadership. With these thoughts in mind, let's turn our attention to six principles of a loving leader.[1]

Principle # 1: Know your wife in order to look out for her welfare. You may be thinking that it's silly for me to even include so basic a principle. How could a man live with a woman without knowing her? However, before you dismiss this principle, consider the following questions:

- What is your wife's greatest concern right now?
- What is her greatest need?
- What is her wildest dream?
- What is her smallest pain?
- What new vista would she like to explore?

If you cannot answer these questions with absolute certainty, then you probably don't know your wife as well as you think, and certainly not well enough to love her as you should.

Principle # 2: Keep the channels of communication open and clear. Real communication can only flourish in an environment of love and trust. Your wife must feel safe with you before she will open up and share her whole heart. Only when she knows that you will really listen to her can she risk the depth of disclosure that produces true marital intimacy.

SIX PRINCIPLES OF A LOVING LEADER

Principle # 3: Set an example. A loving leader models the behavior and values that he desires in his wife and children. For instance, if he wants his wife to share her heart with him, he must open his heart to her. When he practices being transparent and vulnerable, she will be encouraged to respond in kind. The same thing is true for respect, or kindness, or even charity. A loving leader practices these virtues as a way of encouraging them in his wife and children.

Principle # 4: Make sound and timely decisions. A leader's primary responsibility is to lead, and that entails decision making. Unfortunately, there is an increasing number of men who are abdicating this vital responsibility. Some of it has to do with their personalities, but conditioning, I believe, plays a greater role. With the rise of the feminist movement, traditional roles for men have been called into question including decision making. As a result, many men are less sure of themselves, and this is reflected in their inability to make wise and timely decisions.

While this new submissiveness may be welcomed by today's feminist, it is a source of increasing frustration for the Christian woman. She wants her man to be the head of their home — not a tyrant or a dictator, but the loving leader described in Ephesians 5.

How, you may be thinking, can an indecisive man learn to be decisive? While there is no easy answer, there are some disciplines which, if practiced, will provide help and encouragement. In order to make wise and timely decisions, a man should seek the counsel of a trusted Christian brother. He should discuss the situation in depth with his wife, giving careful consideration to her input. Finally, he should ask God for special wisdom. "If any of you lacks wisdom, he should ask God, who gives generously to all without finding fault, and it will be given to him."[2]

Principle # 5: Determine your wife's gifts and capabilities and encourage her accordingly. The gifts and abilities your wife has were given to her by God. Therefore it is vitally important that you encourage your wife to maximize her God–given gifts. Not only will this benefit the Kingdom of God but the family as well, for a fulfilled woman will be a better wife and mother.

Principle # 6: Seek responsibility and take responsibility for your actions. When it's time to do the right thing, time to make tough decisions, it's time for the husband to step forward and assume responsibility. This is true whether it involves a tough parent–teacher conference, or a painful decision regarding the care of an aged parent. A wife shouldn't be expected to make those kinds of decisions alone, no matter how busy her husband is.

And when you make a mistake, be man enough to own it and do what you can to make restitution. I've never known anyone to bat a thousand in decision making, and you probably won't either. It's not important for you to be perfect, but it is critical that you recognize your mistakes and take responsibility for them.

Watergate will probably be remembered as one of the most infamous political scandals in the history of our nation. It was a tragic and unnecessary abuse of power, but it need not have become the destructive and divisive issue it did. "If only Nixon had said he was sorry the country (or most of it) would have most likely forgiven him and let him get on with his presidency."[3] But when he insisted on covering up his part in the conspiracy, the country felt betrayed and lost confidence in his leadership. The same principle applies in our relationship with our wife and children.

ACTION STEPS:
- Memorize the six principles of a loving leader:
  1) Know your wife in order to look out for her welfare.
  2) Keep the channels of communication open and clear.
  3) Set an example.
  4) Make sound and timely decisions.
  5) Determine your wife's gifts and capabilities and encourage her accordingly.
  6) Seek responsibility and take responsibility for your actions.

SIX PRINCIPLES OF A LOVING LEADER

■ On a scale of one to ten, with ten being a perfect score, rate yourself as a loving leader based on these six principles. Give yourself a one to ten rating for each one of the six principles.

■ Now ask your wife to read this chapter and give you a one to ten rating on each one of the six principles. When she is finished, compare your scores. Ask her to suggest specific ways you can improve in these particular areas. Conclude with a time of prayer together.

Thought for the Day:

"Headship is leadership, a leadership of love. It is not a general commanding his army, a computer analyst pushing the right buttons, a master in charge of his slave. It is simply taking our God–given responsibility to care for our wives and families and to lead them in love toward the goals which God has chosen for us."[4]

— Jack Mayhall

Scripture for the Day:

"Two are better than one,
        because they have a good return for
                their work:
If one falls down,
        his friend can help him up.
But pity the man who falls
        and has no one to help him up!
Also, if two lie down together, they
                will keep warm.
        But how can one keep warm alone?
Though one may be overpowered,
        two can defend themselves.
A cord of three strands is not quickly broken."

— Ecclesiastes 4:9–12

CHAPTER 19

THE SPIRITUAL LEADER

lthough the vast majority of Christian husbands would agree that a man has no higher responsibility than to be the spiritual leader of his home, many men have only the vaguest idea of what that really means. In truth, most Christian husbands would be hard pressed to write a job description for the position. And herein lies our problem — we know that God expects us to be the spiritual leaders of our family, but we don't have a clue where to begin.

Let me share three principles which I believe will help you get started:

1) A spiritual leader must minister out of the overflow of his own spiritual life.
2) A spiritual leader must lead by example.
3) A spiritual leader must establish traditions that can be passed from one generation to the next.

Let's consider these one at a time.

Principle # 1: Minister out of the overflow. Being the spiritual leader of your family is something you *are* before it is something you *do*. It goes without saying that you cannot be a spiritual leader of any kind unless you are a spiritual man. Therefore the first duty of a Christian husband and father is to cultivate his personal spiritual life. This can only be accomplished through the consistent practice of spiritual disciplines. Things like prayer, Scripture reading, study, fellowship, worship, and service. The man who makes these disciplines a regular part of his life will grow in the grace and knowledge of the Lord Jesus Christ. And in the process he will equip himself to be the spiritual leader of his family.

Principle # 2: Lead by example. Most of what I know about being the spiritual leader in my home I learned from my father. He wasn't a man much given to words, at least not with us kids. I can't remember a single time when he sat me down and tried to teach me anything. Yet, almost everything I know about life and godliness I learned from him. He taught me how to live, by living a godly life before me.

I've never heard him curse, and I seldom heard him complain, but I did hear him pray a lot. Many a morning I was awakened in the pre–dawn darkness by the sound of his voice drifting in from the living room. Well do I remember slipping out of bed and tip–toeing down the hall to listen as Dad prayed for my mother and us kids. Somehow I felt loved and secure knowing he was praying for us. And when a teenage problem created a momentary crisis in my young life, he was always there. After listening to me pour out my heart, he would say, "Let's pray about it," and we would kneel together on the hardwood floor of the living room and talk to God.

Yet, as far as Dad was concerned, being the spiritual leader of our home was more than just devotions and intercessory prayer. For him it meant being a good steward of our resources and a caring husband. In addition to being a more than adequate mechanic, who serviced and repaired his own cars, Dad was also a willing helper to my mother who had her hands full with four kids. He changed diapers, helped make up beds, washed and dried dishes, and did just about anything else that needed done. From him I learned what it meant to be a servant–leader years before that phrase was coined.

Principle # 3: Establish traditions that can be passed from one generation to the next. In our home, family tradition was established early, and carefully kept. That may sound restrictive to you, but it provided the routine which freed us to enjoy family life with a minimum of hassles. Things like prayer at meal time and church attendance — each and every time the church doors were open — were givens. And since the family routines were clearly defined and carefully kept, there was seldom any reason to challenge them.

Although the spiritual traditions that one generation passes to the next are seldom practiced in exactly the same way, the spiritual values and benefits remain intact. For instance, I seldom pray alone in the living room as my father does, but I have made it a regular habit to drive to the church for early morning prayer. And when Leah was still at home I would often kneel beside her bed after she was asleep and pray for her. Even now when she and her husband face a challenging situation, they often call and we pray together by phone. For Brenda and me, a shared prayer is often the last thing we do before shutting out the light at the end of the day.

I'm forty–six years old now, and I realize that there are many things I may never accomplish. For instance, I may never serve as pastor of a church of several thousand members, and I will probably never be elected to an important position in my denomination.

And that's okay. Achievements of that nature, while gratifying, pale in comparison with the true achievements of life — the shaping of the faith and character of our families.

I'm convinced that when we stand before God, at the final judgment, He will not ask us about our honors and the awards we have won. He will not ask us about the degrees we have earned, or the wealth we have amassed. Rather He will ask, "Where are the children I entrusted to you?"

In light of that, the greatest reward a man could ever hope to receive, this side of eternity, is to see his children cherishing the faith which he entrusted to them. And to watch with thanksgiving as they make the family's spiritual traditions their own and a vital part of their children's lives.

ACTION STEPS:

- Write a detailed job description for the spiritual leader of the family.
- Ask your wife to read this chapter and then write her own job description for the spiritual leader of the family.

THE SPIRITUAL LEADER

- Now compare the two and, using the Scriptures, formulate a job description that you can both agree on.

- Pray together and ask God to enable you to truly become the spiritual leader of your family.

Thought for the Day:

"Late in life Evangeline Booth, age eighty–one and then general of the Salvation Army, was asked when she had first wanted to be a part of the Salvation Army. 'Very early,' she answered. 'I saw my parents [founders of the Salvation Army] working for their people, bearing their burdens. Day and night. They did not have to say a word to me about Christianity.'"[1]

— R. Kent Hughes

Scripture for the Day:

"...As I was with Moses, so I will be with you; I will never leave you or forsake you. Be strong and very courageous. Be careful to obey all the law my servant Moses gave you; do not turn from it to the right or to the left, that you may be successful wherever you go. Do not let this Book of the Law depart from your mouth; mediate on it day and night, so that you may be careful to do everything written in it. Then you will be prosperous and successful. Have I not commanded you? Be strong and courageous. Do not be terrified; do not be discouraged, for the Lord your God will be with you wherever you go."

— Joshua 1:5,7–9

A MAN AND HIS CHILDREN

"I was only twenty–three years old when our daughter, Leah Starr, was born on May 27, 1970. Had I known then what I know now, I would have been terrified! I had no idea that my relationship with Leah would shape her relationship with her heavenly Father. That unconsciously, she would attribute to God the Father the strengths and weaknesses she saw in me, her earthly father. Nor did I realize that my words would forever shape her self–image, giving her confidence to follow her dreams or locking her in a prison of inferiority. I had no idea how important the gift of my presence would be, or how much she would depend upon my counsel and guidance. No, on the day that Leah was born I was too naive to realize that I was embarking on the most important assignment of my life. And that if I failed as a father, all my other achievements would be somehow diminished."

— Richard Exley

CHAPTER 20

MAKING MEMORIES

As I recall my own childhood, the thing I remember most is the special relationship I had with my dad. Thinking about it now, several memories come to mind — the time Dad helped me build a clubhouse when I was maybe ten or eleven years old, the first time he took me deer hunting, and all the times he played catch with me in the evening after supper. Still, no memory is more special than the time he took my brother, Don, and me fishing at the North Sterling Reservoir.

We borrowed Uncle Denny's boat and set out for the reservoir in the pre–dawn darkness. When at last we reached the lake, I could hardly contain my excitement. What could be better than trolling for trout in Colorado? In a matter of minutes we had launched the boat, and while Dad connected the gas line and primed the engine, Don and I began rigging up. Don selected a green and yellow flatfish while I fastened a hot pink daredevil on my line. Distinctly I can recall the mist rising from the water to swallow our boat, waves lapping gently against the bow, the smell of the morning.

I watched as Dad tugged on the pull cord, disrupting the early morning stillness with the abbreviated cough of the outboard engine. It took two more tries before the trolling motor settled into a rattling chug and we began letting our lines out. Within a matter of seconds I had a strike. A fourteen–inch rainbow did a tail dance about twenty feet behind the boat before throwing the hook. Although my excitement was tempered with disappointment I couldn't wait to try again.

Before the morning was done I had caught a nice rainbow trout and two largemouth bass. Still, the thing I remember most is not the fish I caught, or the beauty of the sunrise, but just the chance to be with Dad. And this was just the first of many such trips. Somehow, year after year Dad managed to take us on vacations he couldn't afford to provide, in order to make memories we couldn't afford to be without. Needless to say, my life is the richer for his commitment.

MAKING MEMORIES

ACTION STEPS:

- Take a few minutes now to remember something your father did that made you feel loved and special. For example, my friend Keith and his dad listened to the St. Louis Cardinal's baseball games together on long summer evenings. It was their special time, and he remembers it with deep feeling.

- Examine your own life. Are you spending quality time with your children? Are you doing things with them that make them feel loved and special?

- Make a list of the things you do with your children. Ask God to help you to make those shared times special.

Thought for the Day:

"...as I thought about my own children. I wondered what memories will predominate in their minds when I lie at the point of death, a moment or two from now. What will they remember to be the happiest experiences of their lives? Will they recall a busy father who was preoccupied with writing books and catching planes and answering mail and talking on the telephone and being a 'big man'? Or will they recall a patient dad who took time to love them and teach them and enjoy the beauty of God's world with them? I pray that the Lord will help me keep my little family at the top of my list of priorities during the precious prime-time years."[1]

— Dr. James Dobson

Scripture for the Day:

"Fathers, do not exasperate your children; instead, bring them up in the training and instruction of the Lord."

— Ephesians 6:4

CHAPTER 21

THE GIFT OF YOURSELF

Not infrequently a busy man is tempted to feel that the time spent playing with his children is wasted. Nothing could be further from the truth. Think of your own childhood. Aren't those special times spent with your father a continuing source of strength and encouragement even today? And if you were not fortunate enough to have such a relationship with your father, don't you still feel the loss? In truth, there is nothing you can give your children that will be more lasting or more deeply appreciated than the gift of yourself.

It is said of James Boswell, the famous biographer of Samuel Johnson, that he often referred to a special day in his childhood when his father took him fishing. The day was fixed in his mind, and he often reflected upon many of the things his father had taught him in the course of their fishing experience together.

After having heard of that particular excursion so often, it occurred to someone much later to check the journal that Boswell's father kept to see what he had said about the fishing trip. Turning to that date, the reader found only one sentence: "Gone fishing today with my son; a day wasted."

For the elder Boswell, it seemed a day wasted. For his son, it was a day to be remembered, one which shaped him for the rest of his life!

What am I trying to say? Just this: Life's most valuable lessons are seldom learned in times of formal training. Rather, they are passed from one generation to the next during a shared experience, a mutual project, or a special camping trip. At the time we are seldom aware that anything rare or lasting has happened. It is only later, when we look back, that we realize that something of real significance has occurred.

In light of that fact, let me encourage you to take time to do fun things with your children. Remember, many of life's most profound experiences are unplanned. They are simply the product of time spent together in an atmosphere of love and trust.

THE GIFT OF YOURSELF

ACTION STEPS:

■ See if you can recall some of the things your father taught you. I dare say that they were "caught" more than taught; that is, you learned them while you were sharing a project or an outing with your father. Why not write your dad a note and thank him for those special times?

■ Get your appointment calendar and schedule in time for your children. Make every effort to attend their school activities and their ball games. Your presence means more than you will ever know.

Thought for the Day:

"A young successful attorney said:

'The greatest gift I ever received was a gift I got one Christmas when my dad gave me a small box. Inside was a note saying, "Son, this year I will give you 365 hours, an hour every day after dinner. It's yours. We'll talk about what you want to talk about, we'll go where you want to go, play what you want to play. It will be your hour!"'

'My dad not only kept his promise,' he said, 'but every year he renewed it — and it's the greatest gift I ever had in my life. I am the result of his time.'"[1]

— Moody Monthly

Scripture for the Day:

"Listen, my son, accept what I say,
 and the years of your life will be many.
I guide you in the way of wisdom
 and lead you along straight paths.
When you walk, your steps will not be hampered;
 when you run, you will not stumble.
Hold on to instruction, do not let it go;
 guard it well, for it is your life."

— Proverbs 4:10–13

CHAPTER 22

THE ART OF PARENTING

Parenting isn't easy, but I do believe it is relatively simple, relatively uncomplicated. In addition to food and shelter, every child needs three things: unconditional love, consistent discipline, and spiritual training. If we provide these three essentials, we can be reasonably sure that our children will turn out all right. Deprive them of these fundamentals, and they will struggle with their self–esteem all their lives.

In my work with professional groups I frequently encounter men and women who over–react to the smallest slight, imagined or real. Others are defensive, still others are withdrawn or have trouble relating to persons in authority. More often than not, these difficulties have their roots in the parent–child relationship. Not infrequently such people were deprived of the unconditional love that was needed to enable them to become whole persons.

Unconditional love is exactly that — unconditional. It is not dependent upon the child's performance. It is given freely, consistently, and it enables a child to unconsciously separate his value as a person from his performance, whether good or bad. As a father, you can express your love in a variety of ways, but none is more effective than touching and telling. And remember, little boys need that kind of affection just as much as little girls.

In addition to unconditional love, our children also need consistent discipline. This is a sensitive area and some men get the wrong idea when we talk about disciplining our children. They literally turn their homes into concentration camps. Their children cower in fear. Meal time is akin to roll call at Auschwitz. The smallest infraction becomes a capital offense and is punished accordingly. Day after day their children are forced to eat the bitter bread of humiliation, and as a result, they grow up introverted and hostile.

THE ART OF PARENTING

But that's the farthest thing from godly discipline, which is administered out of love and has the child's well being at heart. Its goal is to prepare him for life. Obedience to parental authority teaches him to submit to God's authority and to those God has placed over him. If this lesson is learned early in his life, he will be spared many painful experiences as he grows into an adult.

In order for discipline to accomplish this goal, however, it must be consistent. The boundaries need to be clearly defined and the consequences appropriate. Children need to know that every time they are disobedient, they will be punished. This is not cruelty but love, tough love.

Discipline without love is tyrannical and produces children who will grow up to be both hostile and afraid. Love without discipline is permissive and trains children to be selfish and obnoxious. But when unconditional love and consistent discipline are combined, they produce children who are emotionally healthy and well adjusted.

The third thing every child needs is spiritual training. You can begin praying for your child even before he is born. The Scriptures teach that God is involved with their lives while they are yet in the womb and even before. Of Jeremiah the Lord said, "'Before I formed you in the womb I knew you, and before you were born I consecrated you....'"[1] And Luke tells us that John the Baptist was filled with the Holy Ghost "...even from birth."[2]

As soon as your wife begins nursing your baby, she can sing spiritual songs to him. As she lovingly rocks him in her arms, the soft lullaby's of God's love will create a sense of warmth and security. Prayers and memorized Scripture verses can also be recited as the two of you lovingly tend him, forever binding the concept of God with the sense of love and security in his mind. Of course, as he grows older more formal training should begin in the form of graduated family devotions. Do this, and you can be sure that your child will grow up to serve the Lord even as you do.

A MAN AND HIS CHILDREN

ACTION STEPS:

- Ask yourself some hard questions:

    1) What specific things do I do to demonstrate my unconditional love for my children? Am I openly affectionate? How often do I tell them how much I love them?

    2) Am I providing consistent and appropriate discipline? Please explain.

    3) Do I pray with my children regularly? How often? Am I teaching them the Word of God?

    4) Am I a good example? Please explain.

- Share your answers with your wife and ask her to give you suggestions on ways in which you can be a better father.

Thought for the Day:

"The terrible fact is, we can either grace our children, or damn them with unrequited wounds which never seem to heal....Men, as fathers you have such power! You will have this terrible power till you die, like it or not — in your attitude toward authority, in your attitude toward women, in your regard for God and the Church. What terrifying responsibilities! This is truly the power of life and death."[3]

— R. Kent Hughes

THE ART OF PARENTING

Scripture for the Day:

"My son, keep your father's commands
    and do not forsake your mother's teaching.
Bind them upon your heart forever;
    fasten them around your neck.
When you walk, they will guide you;
    when you sleep, they will watch over you;
        when you awake, they will speak to you.
For these commands are a lamp,
    this teaching is a light,
and the corrections of discipline
    are the way to life."

— Proverbs 6:20–23

A MAN AND HIS CHILDREN

Chapter 23

THE GIFT OF
SELF–CONFIDENCE

One of my favorite athletes is former Olympic medalist Glenn Cunningham. He was the outstanding miler of his day, setting world records in both the eight–hundred–meters and the mile. I admire him, not simply for his athletic achievements, but for his courage and selflessness. Following his track career he established the Cunningham Youth Ranch where, for thirty years, he and his wife, Ruth, have helped more than nine–thousand troubled young people.

In order to become a world–class athlete, Glen had to overcome almost impossible odds. At the age of seven he was severely burned and the doctor told his parents he would never walk again, let alone run. For months it seemed the doctor's dire prognosis would prove correct. Glen was in constant pain and there was no way he could bend his legs or put any weight on them.

A less determined person might have given up, but not Glen. During those long months of painful rehabilitation he kept replaying his father's words over and over again. "Glen, you are a natural runner. Never quit. Run on." He dreamed of the day he would run again. He visualized himself running in competition —pacing himself for distance, pumping his arms to get more speed, outdistancing his competition.

Months later he was able to hobble across the room, then, after weeks of painful effort, he was able to walk with a limp, finally he was able to run with a hopping gait. After years of pain and frustration, plus lots of exercise, he won his first race at the age of twelve. As he walked home his father's words kept ringing in his ears, "Run on. Never quit."

Where did Glen Cunningham get the courage and faith to overcome such incredible odds? Where did he get the inner strength to go on believing in himself when it seemed all hope was gone? No doubt God and his Christian faith provided invaluable strength, but there was something else too — his father's confidence. His father believed he could do it, and as a result Glen dared to believe in himself. And because he believed in himself, he accomplished the impossible.

ACTION STEPS:

■ Our children tend to get their basic self–image from us, from what we say to them, from what we believe about them. Now replay the things you regularly say to your children and see if you are building their self–confidence or if you are undermining their self–worth.

■ Make a list of the kind of things you shouldn't say to your children. Things like: Can't you ever do anything right? When will you ever learn? You are so irresponsible. Now ask God to set a watch on your lips lest you wound your children with your words.

■ Make a list of the kind of things you should say to children. Things like: I'm so glad you're my son/daughter. You make me so proud when you do that. I love you. Now ask God to help you affirm your children every day.

Thought for the Day:

"How desperately the growing child needs praise, recognition, affirmation. These are aspects of love. A truly loving parent will express approval not only for the child's performance, but for the child himself, as a person. Perhaps once in a hundred years a person may be ruined by excessive praise, but surely once every minute someone dies inside for lack of it."[1]

— Cecil G. Osborne

Scripture for the Day:

"Reckless words pierce like a sword,
but the tongue of the wise brings healing."

— Proverbs 12:18

"The tongue that brings healing is a tree of life,
but a deceitful tongue crushes the spirit."

— Proverbs 15:4

CHAPTER 24

A SACRED TRUST

As a man you have no responsibility more challenging than that of the spiritual training of your children. Both Scripture and history are filled with the tragic accounts of great men who failed in this critical assignment — Eli the priest, Samuel the prophet, and David the king, to name three. According to 1 Samuel, "Eli's sons were wicked men; they had no regard for the Lord."[1] Nor were Samuel's sons any better: "...[they] did not walk in his ways. They turned aside after dishonest gain and accepted bribes and perverted justice."[2]

No one, however, suffered more at the hands of his children than David. His family history reads like a cheap novel. Amnon, David's son, raped his sister Tamar, creating a scandal in the palace. Two years later, Tamar's brother Absalom took his revenge and murdered Amnon. And finally, Absalom led an armed rebellion against his father David, driving him from Jerusalem and breaking his heart.

These were great men, godly men, but their achievements are somehow diminished by their parental failures. Although the Scriptures give us only glimpses of their relationship with their children, it is enough to give us some insight into their parental shortcomings. Eli may have been too permissive: "For I [the Lord] told him that I would judge his family forever because of the sin he knew about; his sons made themselves contemptible, and he failed to restrain them."[3]

Samuel was simply too busy. He apparently gave himself to the work of the Lord at the expense of his relationship with his sons. David's failure, on the other hand, was more overt. He betrayed his children's trust when he committed adultery with Bathsheba and then had her husband murdered. From that moment forward they lost all respect for him.

What can we learn from all of this? Several things, I hope. First, nothing is more important than our children. If we lose them, nothing else really matters. Therefore, we must give them our very best. Second, spiritual training doesn't just happen. We have to work at it with patience and consistency. Third, what we teach by precept must also be taught by example. We must always be careful to live a godly life before our children.

A SACRED TRUST

ACTION STEPS:

■ I identified three possible ways in which these great men may have failed their children — permissiveness, busyness, and moral compromise. Examine your own life and relationship with your children to see if you are guilty of similar failures. If you are, make a list of what you are going to do to rectify them. Be specific.

Thought for the Day:

"Doctor Potter tells the story of a young man who stood at the bar of a court of justice to be sentenced for forgery. The judge had known him from a child, for his father had been a famous legal light and his work on the Law of Trusts was the most exhaustive work on the subject in existence. 'Do you remember your father?' asked the judge sternly, 'that father whom you have disgraced?'

"The prisoner answered: 'I remember him perfectly. When I went to him for advice or companionship, he would look up from his book on the Law of Trusts, and say, "Run away, boy, I am busy." My father finished his book, and here I am.' The great lawyer had neglected his own trust, with awful results."[4]

— T. De Witt Talmadge

Scripture for the Day:

"Teach me, O Lord, to follow your decrees;
    then I will keep them to the end.
Give me understanding, and I will keep your law
    and obey it with all my heart.
Direct me in the path of your commands,
    for there I find delight.
Turn my heart toward your statutes
    and not toward selfish gain.
Turn my eyes away from worthless things;
    renew my life according to your word."

— Psalm 119:33–37

CHAPTER 25

SPIRITUAL TRAINING

As husbands and fathers, most of us realize that God has charged us with the responsibility for our children's spiritual training. Unfortunately, many of us don't have a clue as to how to go about fulfilling that charge. Once we get beyond giving thanks at meals and bedtime prayers we are at a loss. It's not that we don't care, but we simply don't know where to start.

I'm not going to try to give you any hard and fast rules, but I do think I can share some principles which will be helpful.

Principle # 1: Teach your children biblical principles to live by. Through Moses, God told the fathers of Israel, "These commandments that I give you today are to be upon your hearts. Impress them on your children..."[1] Of course, Moses was talking about the whole law of God, but for our purposes let's break it down into three or four concepts.

First, we must teach our children to love God. Jesus said: "'Love the Lord your God with all your heart and with all your soul and with all your mind.' This is the first and greatest commandment. And the second is like it: 'Love your neighbor as yourself.' All the Law and the Prophets hang on these two commandments."[2]

Next, we must teach our children to obey God. The wise man writes: "...Fear God and keep his commandments, for this is the whole duty of man."[3]

Then we must teach our children to trust God. An ancient Proverb declares: "Trust in the Lord with all your heart and lean not on your own understanding; in all your ways acknowledge him, and he will make your paths straight."[4]

Principle # 2: Know your child. Proverbs 22:6 says, "Train a child in the way he should go, and when he is old he will not turn from it." The *New American Standard Bible* footnotes this verse and says the literal translation of "in the way he should go" is "according to his way," or in accordance with the way he is shaped or formed.[5] In other words, every child is unique, and as parents we must discover how our child learns — what drummer he marches to, as it were — and then fit our teaching style to his learning style.

Principle # 3: Strike when the iron is hot. This principle focuses on timing. While there is probably no "wrong" time for sharing spiritual truth, some moments are more conducive to learning than others, and it is a wise father who knows the difference. He will seize those special moments for he realizes they afford him the opportunity to shape his child's worldview.

The old–timers used to call that "striking when the iron is hot." The phrase itself came out of the village blacksmith's shop and referred to that moment when the iron was white hot and capable of being shaped by the blacksmith. It only lasted a moment, and once the iron cooled off it had to be reheated before the blacksmith could finish his work. So it is with a child and spiritual instruction.

In addition to those special moments, spiritual training for our children should also include a regular devotional time. This scheduled instruction — family worship, if you please — sets the spiritual tone. While it may not have as dramatic an impact as one of those "strike when the iron is hot" experiences, its importance cannot be overemphasized. It prepares the child's heart, lays a firm foundation, and establishes a holy habit of spiritual discipline. In truth, the spiritual formation of our children requires both regular instruction and spontaneous moments.

ACTION STEPS:

- If you do not already have a regular family worship time, sit down with your wife and determine when would be the best time for your family.

- Structure your family devotions with the ages of your children in mind. You may want to visit your local Christian bookstore and pick up a *Children's Story Bible* and a book of Bible stories. Remember, it is important to make family worship fun!

- Some of the most important spiritual training your child will ever receive will probably happen spontaneously as you spend time together. That being the case, determine right now, before God, that you will make time with your children your highest priority.

Thought for the Day:

"Men, time is the chrysalis of eternity — there is no other time but the present. I realize we all go through periods in our lives when we have little time for our families — it is part of the natural rhythm of life. But excessive 'busyness' must not be by choice — as it often is! We must beware of packing our schedules by saying 'yes' to things which mean 'no' to our families. Now is the time to take time. There is no other! Will you do it? Will I?"[6]

— R. Kent Hughes

Scripture for the Day:

"These commandments that I give you today are to be upon your hearts. Impress them on your children. Talk about them when you sit at home and when you walk along the road, when you lie down and when you get up. Tie them as symbols on your hands and bind them on your foreheads. Write them on the doorframes of your houses and on your gates."

— Deuteronomy 6:6–9

CHAPTER 26

OWNING OUR MISTAKES

L et's not kid ourselves, we men are not perfect, and sometimes we take our frustrations out on our wives and children. Some of that is probably inevitable, a painful fact of life, but a little of it goes a long way. Indeed, if we are not careful we can wound our relationships beyond repair. Our children are especially vulnerable, and if we repeatedly denigrate them they will be scarred for life.

What, you may be wondering, can you do to rectify your parental outbursts? How can you make up for your reckless words and unchristlike behavior? Nothing is more important than owning your mistakes and apologizing. Let me share a personal incident that I believe illustrates this principle rather well.

The first time our future son–in–law visited in our home, I humiliated our daughter. Leah had made us coffee, and when she went to pour it, she discovered that the handle on the coffee pot was too hot to hold barehanded. Instead of getting a potholder, she grabbed the handiest thing — a kitchen towel with fringe on the ends. When she picked up the coffee pot, the fringe touched the red–hot heating element on the stove and caught on fire. Screaming, she dropped both the burning towel and the coffee pot. Thankfully, she wasn't burned, but we had quite a mess.

Here's where the story takes its most embarrassing turn. I lost control and berated Leah right there in front of Todd. "What were you thinking?" I demanded. "You know better than to use a fringed towel around the stove."

Once I got started, I couldn't seem to quit. "You're lucky you didn't burn the house down." With a few more sarcastic remarks, I reduced her to tears, and she ran from the room.

My wife, Brenda, gave me a look that clearly said, "You are one of the world's most insensitive fathers." Without a word she followed Leah upstairs.

OWNING OUR MISTAKES

I risked a glance at Todd, who sat uncomfortably in the living room, not knowing what to do. A discomfiting silence settled between us, and I went to the kitchen to clean up the mess. By the time I had finished, I knew what I had to do.

Excusing myself, I went upstairs to find Leah. When she heard me coming, she turned her face to the wall and tried to stifle her sobs. Sitting down on the edge of her bed, I put my hand on her trembling shoulder. She seemed to cringe beneath my touch, and I thought my heart would break.

An apology was a must, but I didn't know how to begin. I was tempted to explain my behavior, tempted to say something like: "I'm sorry I lost my temper, but you know better than to use a towel around the stove," or, "I'm sorry I spoke to you like that in front of Todd, but what you did was so uncalled for." Somehow I realized that wasn't an apology but an excuse. It still pointed the finger of blame at Leah.

Finally, I managed to accept full responsibility for my behavior and I said, "There was absolutely no excuse for what I did. Please forgive me. If you will come back downstairs, I will apologize to Todd as well."

Leah graciously forgave me and that emotional scene had a happy ending. But had I been unwilling to own my mistake and make restitution for it, our relationship might have been seriously wounded, perhaps for life.

Apologizing is never easy but it is mandatory, especially within the family. Unfortunately, some fathers refuse to apologize to their children even when they know they are in the wrong. They reason, erroneously, that if they apologize their children will lose respect for them. Not true! In truth, an apology is the best way of restoring lost respect. An added benefit is the object lesson our apology provides. It allows us to show our children how a Christian handles his mistakes.

ACTION STEPS:

■ Ask God to help you take a parental inventory. Carefully examine your relationship with your children, looking for any mistakes you might have made. Once you have identified your mistakes, determine whether you have apologized to your children. If you have not sought their forgiveness yet, do so now. Be careful to accept full responsibility for your mistakes.

■ Examine your mistakes again to see if there seems to be a pattern of behavior. If there is a discernible pattern, ask God to help you deal with your emotions before they get out of hand. Be aware of the attitudes and circumstances that normally precede an inappropriate outburst.

■ You may want to discuss these attitudes and circumstances with your wife to see if she has any helpful insights. When you talk with her, try not to be defensive. Pray together and ask God to help you become the best parents you can be.

Thought for the Day:

"Sin is anything I do, or fail to do, which harms another person; it is anything which I do, or fail to do, which harms me. Sin is failing to do, within my power, what I can to help another. Sin is failure to live in love with God and man."[1]

— Cecil G. Osborne

OWNING OUR MISTAKES

Scripture for the Day:

"Set a guard over my mouth, O Lord;
      keep watch over the door of my lips.
Let not my heart be drawn to what is evil,
      to take part in wicked deeds
with men who are evildoers;
      let me not eat of their delicacies.
Let a righteous man strike me — it is a
                  kindness;
let him rebuke me — it is oil on my
                  head.
My head will not refuse it."

                                    — Psalm 141:3–5

CHAPTER 27

A LETTER FOR LEAH

Several years ago I was flying to Anchorage, Alaska, and the lengthy flight afforded me a few hours to myself. There were no phones to answer, no deadlines to meet, and no one scheduled for counseling. After a couple of hours I began to wind down, and as I did I grew nostalgic and decided to write my daughter a letter. I wrote, in part:

"Dear Leah,

"It's been awhile since I've told you what a special person you are. God has given you the gift of joy and self–confidence. I think you have tremendous people skills, and a real talent for public speaking and drama. Never forget though, that when God gives a person special gifts, He also gives them special responsibilities.

"Always remember:

1) Attitude is everything — it is the one thing no one can ever take from you — the freedom to choose how you are going to feel about any situation.

2) Relationships are the most important things in life. Always be careful to use things and love people.

3) Don't be afraid to fail. Nothing great was ever achieved on the first try.

4) God's will is not inhibiting. It frees you to fulfill your highest potential, while enjoying the most meaningful life possible.

5) If you sin, God always stands ready to forgive.

6) True joy is found in striving for God–given goals, even more than in obtaining them; so dare to dream big dreams, dare to attempt great things for God.

"One last thing: Always remember how much your mother and I love you. There is nothing you can do, no success or achievement, which will ever make us love you more. We love you, not because of what you do, but because of who you are.

"Love, Dad"

I share that with you in order to encourage you to take the time to express your love and affirmation to your children. A telephone call is nice, a card is encouraging, but nothing is more lasting than a personal letter from you. Send it in the mail rather than hand–delivering it. It will have more impact that way.

A LETTER FOR LEAH

ACTION STEPS:
- If you are a new parent, consider compiling your thoughts and impressions in a journal. If possible, record something every week. In the years ahead it will be a treasure to warm your heart and a gift your child will appreciate above all others.
- Jot down some of your favorite memories of your children. Now write a letter to each one of them in which you reminisce about those special times.

Thought for the Day:
"...affection is not much good unless it is expressed. What's more, I have a notion that unexpressed feelings have a tendency to shrink, wither, and ultimately die. Putting an emotion into words gives it a life and a reality that otherwise it doesn't have....Similarly, expressing confidence in a person's ability to accomplish something actually strengthens that ability."[1]

— Arthur Gordon

Scripture for the Day:
"Then he said, 'My son, bring me some of your game to eat, so that I may give you my blessing.'

"Jacob brought it to him and he ate; and he brought some wine and he drank. Then his father Isaac said to him, 'Come here, my son, and kiss me.'

"So he went to him and kissed him. When Isaac caught the smell of his clothes, he blessed him and said,

'Ah, the smell of my son
            is like the smell of a field that the Lord has blessed.
May God give you of heaven's dew
            and of earth's richness —
            an abundance of grain and new wine.
May nations serve you
            and peoples bow down to you.
Be lord over your brothers,
            and may the sons of your mother bow down to you.
May those who curse you be cursed
            and those who bless you be blessed.' "

— Genesis 27:25–29

A MAN AND HIS FRIENDS

"Behind Albrecht Durer's famous etching, "Praying Hands," is the story of two friends. "Albrecht Durer and Franz Knigstein were very poor and had to work to support themselves, training as artists in their spare time. However, their manual work was too demanding to allow them proper training.

"In desperation, they at last decided that they should cast lots to decide which of them should carry on working to support the other in art school. Albrecht won the toss, so he went off to spend time with famous artists in training, while Franz worked extra hard to support them both.

"Eventually, Albrecht returned to relieve his friend. Because he had become successful as an artist, he would now be able to send Franz off to the school. But to his horror, Albrecht discovered that the heavy manual work had ruined Franz's hands for ever. Franz would never now be able to become an artist. He had forfeited his own artistic future out of loyalty to his friend.

"One day, Albrecht found Franz on his knees, his hands clasped in prayer, gnarled and yet offered to God in loving sacrifice. Hurriedly, Durer sketched the moment and produced a symbol for the meaning of prayer."[1]

— James Houston

CHAPTER 28

MY FIRST FRIEND

Grandma Miller was my first friend and as I think about her now she seems like something out of *Reader's Digest's* most unforgettable characters. She was born in 1885 in a small village in Iowa, to a poor, but hard–working family. Her parents had little use for what they called "book learnin'." As a consequence she never learned to read or write, and could barely scribble her own name. Her entire life was lived on the ragged edge of poverty, but she was rich in spirit.

I was always welcome in her world — a world of braided rag rugs, coal oil stoves, kerosine lamps, and friends from "the old country." She introduced me to coffee, diluted with thick country cream, before I started school. And sitting at her breakfast table, sipping coffee with Grandpa, I felt like a grown–up long before I had any right to. To this day, a steaming cup of cream–colored coffee can take me back to Grandma's house and the special friendship we shared.

When I was ten, Grandpa died and I began spending four and five nights a week with Grandma. After dark we lit the kerosine lamps and talked for hours. I can't remember much of what we said, no special words of wisdom, but I do remember feeling loved. Grandma accepted me unconditionally and in her presence I never had to be afraid of being judged or rejected. She guided me, she modeled her values for me, but she never tried to change me. Instead, she encouraged me to become the unique person God had created me to be.

As I think about it now, I realize that Grandma accepted me as her peer while allowing me to be a child when I needed to be one. Because of her, I had the best of both worlds — adult company and acceptance, plus the freedom of childhood.

Although she has been dead for nearly thirty years now, she lives on in my memory, and her influence shapes me still. She believed in me and taught me to believe in myself. She was tenacious, and from her example I learned to hang tough and finish what I started. She was a true friend and I am who I am today, at least in part, because of her friendship.

MY FIRST FRIEND

ACTION STEPS:

- Take a few minutes right now and remember your first friend, or the best friend you've ever had. Recall the joy of that friendship. Remember a special event or experience you shared. Now thank God for the gift of friendship.

- Examine that friendship. How did it begin? What was it built on? Be very specific. See if you can identify four or five characteristics — things like mutual interests, shared experiences, trust, etc.

- In order to enhance your present friendships, you may want to make a special effort to incorporate into them some of those same principles.

Thought for the Day:

"To have someone who wants to absorb us, who wants to understand the shape and structure of our lives, who will listen for more than our words, is one of friendship's greatest gifts."[2]

— Paul D. Robbins

Scripture for the Day:

"...Jonathan became one in spirit with David, and he loved him as himself."

— 1 Samuel 18:1

CHAPTER 29

A SPECIAL FRIEND

Years ago, nearly twenty now, when being a writer was just a secret dream, I read the *Journal of a Novel* by John Steinbeck. While writing *East of Eden*, Steinbeck began each day's work with a letter to Pascal Covici, his friend and editor. Those letters served to warm him up for his day's work and have become a kind of commentary on the novel itself. Anyway, I can distinctly remember hoping that someday I might have a relationship like that. A friend who shared my love for books and my passion for writing. Someone with whom I could discuss my day's work, and receive both affirmation and constructive suggestions.

When I began writing for Honor Books, God gave me such a friend — Keith Provance, the general manager. I remember the first time he and his wife, Megan, had dinner with Brenda and me. After the meal we all retired to my study, and I read a story called "Beautiful Dreamer," by Arthur Gordon, in which he told of encountering the generosity of friendship in a most unexpected place. The symbol of that generosity of spirit was a battered old music box which played only one tune — Stephen Foster's haunting melody, "Beautiful Dreamer." Little did I realize how profoundly that story would affect Keith.

Three years later, at Christmas, he presented me with a musical ornament which played "Beautiful Dreamer," and a letter in which he wrote: "This gift is the spoil of a three–year quest which has taken me to many nooks and crannies in several states. Its possession has become a crusade for me, making its significance and meaning even more special, and more worthy of the cause for which it is given.

"Three years ago your friendship dawned a new era in my life. May this small gift, which is a symbol of its beginning, become a treasured possession as your friendship has become to me."

As much as we value our friendship, Keith and I aren't what you would call "buddies," and seldom do we do things together. We are both very busy and we often go weeks at a time without so much as a phone call, but the bond of our friendship remains. Why? Because it is built on our shared faith in Jesus Christ, our mutual appreciation for the written word, and a common commitment to advance the Kingdom, not to mention the ability to celebrate one another's achievements as if they were our own.

A SPECIAL FRIEND

Having read this brief chapter you may be tempted to pray, "Lord, give me a friend like that." Instead, let me suggest that you pray, "Lord, make me a friend like that."

ACTION STEPS:

■ The real secret to having friends is being a friend. Think of the people you are drawn to. Aren't they the kind of people who give freely of themselves without expecting anything in return, without making you feel in their debt? Now ask God to help you be a friend like that.

■ Some expressions of friendship are truly spontaneous, but many of them aren't. Instead, they are the product of caring and careful planning. Take a few minutes now and think of four or five special things that you can do for your friends. Make specific plans for putting your ideas into action.

Thought for the Day:

"People who have warm friends are healthier and happier than those who have none. A single real friend is a treasure worth more than gold or precious stones. Money can buy many things, good and evil. All the wealth of the world could not buy you a friend or pay you for the loss of one."[1]

— C. D. Prentice

"A true friend is one who hears and understands when you share your deepest feelings. He supports you when you are struggling; he corrects you, gently and with love, when you err; and he forgives you when you fail. A true friend prods you to personal growth, stretches you to your full potential. And most amazing of all, he celebrates your successes as if they were his own."[2]

— Richard Exley

Scripture for the Day:

"While David was at Horesh in the Desert of Ziph, he learned that Saul had come out to take his life. And Saul's son Jonathan went to David at Horesh and helped him find strength in God. 'Don't be afraid,' he said. 'My father Saul will not lay a hand on you. You will be king over Israel, and I will be second to you. Even my father Saul knows this.' The two of them made a covenant before the Lord. Then Jonathan went home, but David remained at Horesh."

— 1 Samuel 23:15–18

CHAPTER 30

JONATHAN AND DAVID

If you are like most men, you probably have a number of associates, people with whom you do things, but very few real friends. As sad as that is, it isn't really surprising. From childhood we have been taught to be competitive rather than intimate, to see our associates as rivals rather than potential friends. As a result our relationships are generally superficial. We do things together; we talk about politics, business, sports, even religion, but we don't share our feelings. We don't reveal our real selves.

Jonathan and David show us how to relate, man to man, on a different level. "After David had finished talking with Saul, Jonathan became one in spirit with David, and he loved him as himself. And Jonathan made a covenant with David because he loved him as himself. Jonathan took off the robe he was wearing and gave it to David, along with his tunic, and even his sword, his bow and his belt."[1]

There are several things we can learn from Jonathan and David's relationship that can enable us to build better friendships.

Principle # 1: Recognize the chemistry of friendship. Their friendship was a gift first and then a discipline. Neither Jonathan nor David decided to become friends. It just happened! "...Jonathan became one in spirit with David...."[2]

Principle # 2: Risk the commitment of friendship. "And Jonathan made a covenant with David because he loved him as himself."[3] This covenant was the formalizing of their commitment one to the other, and it would be renewed again and again. It was this covenant — this commitment to the relationship at all costs — which enabled their friendship to survive the jealousy of Jonathan's father Saul, and his determined attempts to take David's life.

Principle # 3: Be willing to make yourself transparent and vulnerable. When Jonathan disrobed, he made himself transparent to David. It was his way of saying that he had nothing to hide, that he wanted David to know the real Jonathan. A friendship built on anything else is just a sham — a make–believe friendship between two people who are pretending to be something other than who they really are. As C. S. Lewis said, "Eros will have naked bodies; friendships naked personalities."[4]

When Jonathan gave David his weapons — his sword, his bow, and his belt — he made himself vulnerable. He was at David's mercy. He had no way to defend himself. So it is in a true friendship. When we share our deepest self with our friend, we are giving him weapons with which he can destroy us. It is the ultimate act of trust, and it is what distinguishes the truly great friendships from those that are just average.

JONATHAN AND DAVID

Principle # 4: Demonstrate selflessness by preferring your friend before yourself. When Jonathan gave David his royal robe, it was a symbolic gesture depicting his willingness to give up his right to the throne. A right which he would renounce in favor of David again and again. " 'Don't be afraid,' he said. 'My father Saul will not lay a hand on you. You will be king over Israel, and I will be second to you....' "[5]

The measure of Jonathan's commitment to David was his willingness to give up the throne that was rightfully his. The measure of David's commitment to Jonathan was his unwillingness to do anything to make the throne his own. They were both selfless in their love one for the other, and thus their friendship has become the standard by which all friendships are judged.

ACTION STEPS:

■ Memorize the four principles which were foundational to Jonathan and David's friendship:

1) Recognize the chemistry of friendship.
2) Risk the commitment of friendship.
3) Be willing to make yourself transparent and vulnerable.
4) Demonstrate selflessness by preferring your friend before yourself.

■ Examine your most important friendships to determine what principles they are built upon. If they do not include the principles that were foundational to Jonathan and David's friendship, determine right now that you are going to make a conscientious effort to incorporate them.

■ Share this chapter with one of your special friends and then discuss it together.

Thought for the Day:

"If surveys of American adults, particularly males, are any indication, friends become a rarer commodity as the years go by....Many of us are forced to treasure the few we have and become less optimistic, frighteningly skeptical about making new ones. It becomes a fearful process to bare bruised feelings and memories to strangers — the very process that establishes fellowship."[6]

— Terry C. Muck

Scripture for the Day:

" 'But show me unfailing kindness like that of the Lord as long as I live, so that I may not be killed, and do not ever cut off your kindness from my family — not even when the Lord has cut off every one of David's enemies from the face of the earth.' So Jonathan made a covenant with the house of David, saying, 'May the Lord call David's enemies to account.' And Jonathan had David reaffirm his oath out of love for him, because he loved him as he loved himself."

—1 Samuel 20:14–17

CHAPTER 31

THE POWER OF A FRIEND

I n 1791 William Wilberforce was facing yet another discouraging defeat in his attempt to abolish Britain's slave trade, when he received a letter from John Wesley. That, now famous, letter would prove to be a continuing source of strength for the rest of his life. It read:

"London, February 26, 1791

"Dear Sir:

"Unless the divine power has raised you up...I see not how you can go through your glorious enterprise, in opposing that execrable villainy, which is the scandal of religion, of England, and of human nature. Unless God has raised you up for this very thing, you will be worn out by the opposition of men and devils. But, 'if God be for you, who can be against you?' Are all of them stronger than God? O 'be not weary in well doing!' Go on, in the name of God and in the power of His might, till even American slavery (the vilest that ever saw the sun) shall vanish away before it.

"...That He who has guided you from your youth up, may continue to strengthen you in this and all things, is the prayer of,

"Your affectionate servant,

"J. Wesley."[1]

Four days after writing that letter, Wesley was dead and once again Wilberforce was defeated when the vote was taken in Parliament. He would ultimately prevail in his just and holy cause. During the intervening years, however, he faced innumerable disappointments and was tempted to give up the fight more than once. He was vilified in published articles and victimized in vicious whispering campaigns. His opponents arranged for him to be challenged to a duel and even attempted to kill him, but he would not be deterred.

And every time he became discouraged, he returned to Wesley's letter. Each time he read it, it was like the first time. Never did it fail to encourage and strengthen him.

Finally in 1806, after working tirelessly for twenty years, Wilberforce succeeded in getting a bill passed which abolished the slave trade. Twenty–eight years later, on July 31, 1834, slavery itself was outlawed throughout the British Empire, freeing approximately 800,000 slaves. Although he did not live to see the realization of his dream, having died on August 5, 1833, no one was more responsible than William Wilberforce for the demise of slavery in the British Empire.

Wilberforce died one of the most esteemed men of his day and was buried in the famed Westminster Abbey. His epitaph reads in part:

> "Eminent as he was in every department of public labour,
>   And a leader in every work of charity,
> Whether to relieve the temporal or the spiritual wants
>   of his fellow men
> His name will ever be specially identified
>   With those exertions
> Which, by the blessing of God, removed from England
>   The guilt of the African slave trade,
> And prepared the way for the abolition of slavery
>   in every colony of the Empire."[2]

To that end Wilberforce had devoted his entire life and political career. Yet he might not have prevailed had it not been for the encouragement of his friends who strengthened him in the Lord.

ACTION STEPS:

■ Can you remember a time when someone encouraged you, when they strengthened you in the Lord and enabled you to remain faithful to your appointed task? If so, take a few minutes right now and write them a note expressing your appreciation for their encouragement. Before you mail it, spend a few minutes in prayer thanking God for them and asking Him to bless them.

■ What about your friends? Are any of them facing discouragement or hardship right now? The most helpful thing you can do is pray, but in addition to your prayers look for ways to encourage them. Remember the ways in which others have strengthened you and follow their example.

Thought for the Day:

"Unless we are particularly heroic or saintly persons, each of us needs a relationship with at least one other person who also seeks and trusts the simple way, the Simple Presence. Such a 'spiritual friend' can be enormously supportive to us, and we to them. Even if you meet or write to each other only once a month, it can be enough. Just knowing that someone else is struggling for the simple way with you, whether or not you speak together often, is encouraging. You feel a little less alone, a little less tempted to fall mindlessly into complicating traps. Someone else is there who knows whether or not you are trying to pay attention to the simple way; that brings a kind of accountability that is important. When someone else knows and cares, then we pay that much more attention to what we're doing."[3]

— Tilden H. Edwards

THE POWER OF A FRIEND

Scripture for the Day:

"For when we came into Macedonia, this body of ours had no rest, but we were harassed at every turn — conflicts on the outside, fears within. But God, who comforts the downcast, comforted us by the coming of Titus, and not only by his coming but also by the comfort you had given him. He told us about your longing for me, your deep sorrow, your ardent concern for me, so that my joy was greater than ever."

— 2 Corinthians 7:5–7

A MAN AND HIS MONEY

"**M**oney is really another pair of feet to walk where Christ would walk, money is another pair of hands to heal and feed and bless the desperate families of the earth. In other words, money is my other self. Money can go where I do not have time to go, where I do not have a passport to go. My money can go in my place and heal and bless and feed and help. A man's money is an extension of himself."[1]

— Bruce Larson

CHAPTER 32

FALSE SECURITY

The famous Edgewater Beach Hotel in Chicago was the site of a 1923 meeting of some of the world's most powerful financiers. In attendance was Charles Schwab — the president of the largest independent steel company, Samuel Insull — the president of the largest utility company, Howard Hopson — the president of the largest gas company, Arthur Cutten — the greatest wheat speculator, Richard Whitney — the president of the New York Stock Exchange, Albert Fall — a member of the president's Cabinet, Jesse Livermore — the greatest bear on Wall Street, Leon Fraser — the president of the Bank of International Settlement, and Ivar Kreuger — the head of the world's greatest monopoly. Collectively they controlled more wealth than there was in the United States Treasury.

Yet, for all their financial expertise, theirs is not a pleasant story, for they each came to a bitter end. After living on borrowed money for the last five years of his life, Schwab died penniless. Insull too died destitute, a fugitive from justice and in a foreign country. Insanity claimed Hopson, while Cutten died abroad, insolvent. Both Richard Whitney and Albert Fall ended up in prison, while Livermore, Fraser, and Kreuger all committed suicide.[2]

Although the details of their disastrous demise vary from individual to individual, the similarities give us reason to pause and consider. They were addicted to wealth and the power it represented, and in the end this was their undoing. Had they heeded the scriptural warnings about materialism, they might have escaped their tragic fate.

As men, we should ask ourselves what we can learn from their experience. Remember, he who does not learn from the past is doomed to repeat it. With this in mind, let's turn our attention to the Scriptures to see what they have to say about a man and his money.

FALSE SECURITY

One: The Bible teaches us not to put our confidence in material things, but in God. "Command those who are rich in this present world not to be arrogant nor to put their hope in wealth, which is so uncertain, but to put their hope in God, who richly provides us with everything for our enjoyment."[3]

Two: The Bible warns us of the seductive power of money and its inherit danger. "People who want to get rich fall into temptation and a trap and into many foolish and harmful desires that plunge men into ruin and destruction. For the love of money is a root of all kinds of evil. Some people, eager for money, have wandered from the faith and pierced themselves with many griefs."[4]

Three: The Bible commands us to seek first the Kingdom of God. " 'Therefore I tell you, do not worry about your life, what you will eat or drink; or about your body, what you will wear.... For the pagans run after all these things, and your heavenly Father knows that you need them. But seek first his kingdom and his righteousness, and all these things will be given to you as well.' "[5]

Four: The Bible teaches that the only way to overcome our greedy materialism is to give regularly and sacrificially. "Command them to do good, to be rich in good deeds, and to be generous and willing to share. In this way they will lay up treasure for themselves as a firm foundation for the coming age, so that they may take hold of the life that is truly life."[6]

Five: The Bible teaches that receiving is a consequence of giving, but not a goal. "Give, and it will be given to you. A good measure, pressed down, shaken together and running over, will be poured into your lap. For with the measure you use, it will be measured to you."[7]

A MAN AND HIS MONEY

ACTION STEPS:

- Write a theology of money, that is, what you believe the Bible teaches about a man and his money.

- Compare your theology with the five principles listed in this chapter.

- Now compare your check register with your theology. Are you living by your theology? It has been said that a man's checkbook, more than his theology, tells what he really believes about stewardship.

Thought for the Day:

"I remember Bishop Edwin Holt Hughes telling about being entertained by a wealthy landowner. He had preached in his host's church that morning on God's ownership. Looking over his broad acres and remembering the morning sermon, the man asked, 'Do you mean to tell me, Bishop, that this land does not belong to me?' The bishop said the answer came to him in a flash, 'Ask me that one hundred years from now.'"[8]

— Bruce Larson

FALSE SECURITY

Scripture for the Day:

"Then he said to them, 'Watch out! Be on your guard against all kinds of greed; a man's life does not consist in the abundance of his possessions.'

"And he told them this parable: 'The ground of a certain rich man produced a good crop. He thought to himself, "What shall I do? I have no place to store my crops."

"'Then he said, "This is what I'll do. I will tear down my barns and build bigger ones, and there I will store all my grain and my goods. And I'll say to myself, 'You have plenty of good things laid up for many years. Take life easy; eat, drink and be merry.'"

"'But God said to him, "You fool! This very night your life will be demanded from you. Then who will get what you have prepared for yourself?"

"'This is how it will be with anyone who stores up things for himself but is not rich toward God.'"

— Luke 12:16–21

CHAPTER 33

FOUR LEVELS OF GIVING

artin Luther astutely observed, "There are three conversions necessary: the conversion of the heart, mind, and the purse."[1] For modern man I sometimes think the third is the hardest. He doesn't want anyone — not his wife, not his church, not even God — telling him what to do with his money. If you think I am overstating the case, just observe how tense things get the next time your pastor starts talking about money. In truth, as long as we are defensive about money we have not fully experienced Martin Luther's third conversion.

The conversion of a man's purse is not an event as much as it is a process, a series of small occurrences, each one leading to the next. It starts when we acknowledge that God has a right to ask us to give, and it is complete when we realize that we are just stewards and everything we have is God's. In other words, the management of the financial resources entrusted to us must be done according to scriptural principles and not according to the materialism of the age or the dictates of our personal desires.

The most basic element of stewardship is giving, so let's begin there. Some years ago my friend, Jack Strom, introduced me to the four levels of scriptural giving:

1) Regular giving,

2) Reasoned giving,

3) Revelation giving,

4) Reflected giving.

Regular giving refers to the tithe. "'A tithe of everything from the land, whether grain from the soil or fruit from the trees, belongs to the Lord; it is holy to the Lord. The entire tithe of the herd and flock — every tenth animal that passes under the shepherd's rod — will be holy to the Lord.'"[2]

Paul builds on this same principle in the New Testament when he tells the Corinthian believers, "On the first day of every week, each one of you should set aside a sum of money in keeping with his income...."[3]

Reasoned giving refers to offerings which are above and beyond the tithe. In my own life this means the special offerings I give each week toward the support of missionaries around the world and to the benevolence fund of our local church. It too is regular giving since I do it every week. But it is also reasoned giving because it exceeds the tithe and God allows me to use "reason" to decide how much I can afford to give.

Revelation giving is Spirit–directed and it goes a step further. It often exceeds what reason tells us we can afford to give. It's a man's response to the leading of the Holy Spirit in regard to a specific need. For instance, when a prophet named Agabus, "...stood up and through the Spirit predicted that a severe famine would spread over the entire Roman world....The disciples, each according to his ability, decided to provide help for the brothers living in Judea."[4]

As we have already noted, revelation giving often goes beyond what we are able to give. In this kind of giving no one exceeded the Macedonians. Of them Paul writes, "Out of the most severe trial, their overflowing joy and their extreme poverty welled up in rich generosity. For I testify that they gave as much as they were able, and even beyond their ability...."[5]

Reflected giving refers to the power one man's generosity has to inspire others to give. Paul uses this principle in 2 Corinthians 8 when he tells the Corinthian believers about the generosity of the Macedonians. Then he turns around in Chapter 9 and says that the reason the Macedonian churches gave so much was because "...your [the Corinthians'] enthusiasm has stirred most of them to action."[6]

A MAN AND HIS MONEY

A dear friend of mine gives 60 percent of his gross income to the work of the Lord. He is not a successful businessman, nor is he wealthy. In fact, there are some months when there is not enough money to go around. When that happens, he gets down on his knees and asks God to provide in a supernatural way. Then he mails out the checks that go to the work of the Lord and waits for God to provide the rest so he can pay his monthly bills.

Needless to say, his example has been both a challenge and an inspiration to me. I only pray that my generosity may be used of the Lord to inspire others as well.

ACTION STEPS:

- Has your purse been converted to the Lord? If you answered yes, what evidence can you offer? If you answered no, will you surrender it to the Lord right now?

- Examine your giving and determine which of the four levels best characterize your giving habits. The more mature you become in this area of your spiritual life, the more you will see all four of these levels manifest in your stewardship. Pray now and ask God to increase your faith so you can give more.

- If there is absolutely no way that you can give a full tithe (10 percent of your gross income) in your present circumstances, then give as much as you possibly can and do it regularly. Ask God to bless your faithfulness and promise Him that as He enables you, you will increase your giving.

FOUR LEVELS OF GIVING

Thought for the Day:

"If our expenditure on comforts, luxuries, amusements, etc., is up to the standard common among those with the same income as our own, we are probably giving away too little. If our charities do not at all pinch or hamper us, I should say they are too small. There ought to be things we should like to do and cannot do because our charitable expenditure excludes them."[7]

— C. S. Lewis

Scripture for the Day:

"Each man should give what he has decided in his heart to give, not reluctantly or under compulsion, for God loves a cheerful giver. And God is able to make all grace abound to you, so that in all things at all times, having all that you need, you will abound in every good work. As it is written:

'He has scattered abroad his gifts to

the poor;

his righteousness endures forever.'

You will be made rich in every way so that you can be generous on every occasion, and through us your generosity will result in thanksgiving to God."

— 2 Corinthians 9:7–9,11

CHAPTER 34

WHERE YOUR TREASURE IS

John R. Church, an eccentric Methodist minister of a generation ago, told of accepting his first pastorate. He was just a young man and shortly after he assumed his duties one of the deacons took him aside for a kind of fatherly chat. "Pastor," the elderly deacon said, not unkindly, "you are a gifted young man and you will go a long way in the ministry if you can avoid a few rather common pitfalls."

Leaning forward, speaking in a confidential tone, he continued, "Many a fine young man has ruined his ministry by preaching about money." When John frowned, somewhat puzzled, the old deacon explained, "Churches never have money problems, son, just spiritual problems. If you will preach the 'book' and not go to meddlin' in other folk's private affairs, everything will be just fine. Just fine."

Being a fiery young man of more courage than wisdom, John replied, "You are right, sir, when you say that a church's financial problems are spiritual rather than monetary. And that's exactly why I'm going to preach about money."

The old gent was obviously well intended but, like many a man, poorly informed when it came to what the Bible teaches about money. Apparently he didn't realize that Jesus talked more about money than any other single subject. In the Gospels an average of one out of every ten verses — 288 in all — deal directly with the subject. Sixteen of our Lord's thirty–eight parables address the same issue. The Bible offers approximately five hundred verses on prayer, less than five hundred verses on faith, but more than two thousand verses on money and possessions.

Confronted with that kind of evidence, we should ask ourselves: What is God trying to tell us? I believe the answer can be found in a single verse of Scripture: "'For where your treasure is, there your heart will be also.'"[1] In other words, if God can get a man's money, He will get his heart.

Let me illustrate: I knew a man, some years ago, who came into a small inheritance — less than ten thousand dollars. For the first time in his life he secured the services of a stock broker and invested his entire inheritance in the stock market. Every day thereafter the first thing he read in the newspaper was the stock market report. Before he had invested he could not have cared less, but now the daily stock market report was more important than the headlines.

Now apply that same principle to the Kingdom of God. If God can get a man to put his money into the Church, then it's only a matter of time until that man will become committed to the Church. "'For where your treasure is, there your heart

WHERE YOUR TREASURE IS

will be also.' "[2] If God can get a man to give significantly to the work of missions, it won't be long until that same man will have a burden and a vision for world missions. "'For where your treasure is, there your heart will be also.'"[3]

God did not choose to fund the work of the Kingdom on tithes and offerings because He was running short on cash, but because it was the surest way to get us involved in what He is doing. "'For where your treasure is, there your heart will be also.'"[4]

And the old deacon was right. When we think more about earthly things than eternal things, that's a spiritual problem not a monetary one. But it is a spiritual problem with a monetary answer. "'For where your treasure is, there your heart will be also.'"[5]

ACTION STEPS:

- In order to see where your heart really is, get out your check register and a calculator. Break your expenditures into some broad categories: 1) mortgage payment or rent, 2) utilities, 3) car payment, 4) groceries, 5) clothing, 6) entertainment, and 7) contributions. Your contributions should exceed all categories with the exception of your mortgage payment and perhaps your car payment. If that is not the case for you, then develop a plan to reduce your expenditures while increasing your giving.

Thought for the Day:

"It is easy to surrender part when we have already given the whole. This was shown in the life of a young Norwegian named Peter Torjesen when at the age of seventeen his heart was so stirred by a challenge to missionary giving that he opened his wallet and poured all his money into the offering. As an afterthought he also included a scrap of paper on which he wrote 'Og mit liv' ('And my life'). Significantly, young Torjesen went on to lead a fruitful life as a missionary in China."[6]

— R. Kent Hughes

Scripture for the Day:

"And now, brothers, we want you to know about the grace that God has given the Macedonian churches. Out of the most severe trial, their overflowing joy and their extreme poverty welled up in rich generosity. For I testify that they gave as much as they were able, and even beyond their ability. Entirely on their own, they urgently pleaded with us for the privilege of sharing in this service to the saints. But just as you excel in everything — in faith, in speech, in knowledge, in complete earnestness and in your love for us — see that you also excel in this grace of giving."

— 2 Corinthians 8:1–4,7

CHAPTER 35

LITTLE IS MUCH

T**he economy of the Kingdom operates on the currency of faith rather than monetary value. In other words, the power of our gift for Kingdom good is in direct proportion to the amount of faith required to give. That's why Jesus could say that the widow's two mites equaled more than all the other gifts combined. "'They all gave out of their wealth; but she, out of her poverty, put in everything — all she had to live on.'"[1] It required little or no faith for the wealthy to give out of their abundance, but it required great faith for the widow to give out of her need.**

A second way God determines the Kingdom potential of our gift is to measure what we have given by what we have left. In truth, the power of a man's gift is determined, not by how much he gives, but by how much he keeps. God can do more with a "little" when it is our all than He can with a "lot" when it is but a small portion of what we have.

At least three things happen when a man gives out of his need. First, using both his money and his faith, God ministers to a lost and dying world. His money becomes ministry — it becomes a printing press producing Bibles; it becomes air fare carrying missionaries to the ends of the earth; it becomes Gospel literature telling the story of Jesus to those who have never heard; it becomes a Bible school for training national pastors; it becomes a church building for an indigenous congregation; it becomes provision for the missionary and his family; and it becomes the grace of God to a needy world!

Next, God credits his gift of faith and the ministry it produces to his eternal account. As Paul told the Macedonians, "...in the early days of your acquaintance with the gospel, when I set out from Macedonia, not one church shared with me in the matter of giving and receiving, except you only; for even when I was in Thessalonica, you sent me aid again and again when I was in need. Not that I am looking for a gift, but I am looking for what may be credited to your account."[2]

Although those first–century believers could not travel with Paul, nor share in his ministry, they were still able to have a part through their gifts. And in eternity they will share in Paul's missionary reward!

LITTLE IS MUCH

Based on this scriptural principle, I can say confidently that, although I have never ministered in Africa, I will have an African reward. Why? Because I have faithfully supported several missionaries to Africa, and God is crediting a small portion of their work to my eternal account.

I have never ministered in India, but through missionary, David Grant, and others I have had a part in what God is doing in that country as well. I have never been to China, but through my involvement with University Language Services, and my gifts to Kevin and Karen Hardin, a small portion of the work there is being credited to my eternal account. Nor have I ever been to Russia, but for years I have supported Beverly Schmidgal, Jim and Dolly Gilbert, and a number of others who have been used in special ways in the great revival that is taking place there. This too has been credited to my eternal account.

Through our faith gifts to world missions we all become missionaries sharing in the eternal reward!

And finally, God uses a person's act of faith as a way to supply his personal needs. Paul says, "And my God will meet all your needs according to his glorious riches in Christ Jesus."[3] This is not an unconditional promise made to everyone, but a special promise to those who have given sacrificially to world missions.

When I became pastor of Christian Chapel in Tulsa, Oklahoma, in 1980, the church had defaulted on nearly $750,000 of indebtedness and was facing a foreclosure. After some months I felt the Holy Spirit was asking the congregation to take a step of faith and make world missions their first priority. When I presented my vision to the official board, God quickened it to their hearts.

To make that vision a reality required several steps: 1) We amended our constitution and by-laws to reflect our commitment to world missions. 2) We made a "faith promise" to increase our monthly missions giving by five hundred dollars every quarter. 3) We agreed to develop a missionary-in-residence program in which the church would provide a fully furnished home at no cost to the missionary for his use when he was home on furlough. In addition we would provide a minimum monthly pledge for him of a thousand dollars.

A MAN AND HIS MONEY

At the time these commitments seemed almost ludicrous. Our congregation barely numbered one hundred and we were worshipping in a rented junior high school auditorium. We were in default on debts of nearly $750,000 and our annual income was just over $125,000. Nonetheless, like the Macedonian churches, we made a faith commitment out of our most severe trial and extreme poverty.

Almost immediately God began to supply our needs in supernatural ways. A piece of undeveloped property suddenly sold, and we were able to pay off all our indebtedness. A man heard about our vision to provide a missionary–in–residence home, and he offered to buy a house for it. Three months later we closed on a beautiful two–thousand–square–foot home, debt free. Another man gave Christian Chapel a thirty–thousand–dollar Christmas gift. The really big miracle, however, happened fourteen months after our decision to make missions our first priority. In August 1982 some stock in an oil company was sold in the church's name and we received a check for $429,444.79!

Since 1982 our congregation has grown to nearly a thousand members. We were able to purchase 8.7 acres of land and build a facility of our own. In the ensuing ten years we have given nearly $2 million to world missions and have sent scores of people from our congregation into missions work. Truly God has supplied all of our needs "...according to his glorious riches in Christ Jesus."[4]

ACTION STEPS:

- On a scale of one to ten, with ten being the highest, how would you rate your stewardship? Don't measure yourself against others but rather measure yourself against the teachings of God's Word. Is there any area of your life in which you are deliberately living beneath your means in order to give more to the work of the Lord?

- What specific steps can you take to become a better steward?

- As a faithful steward you can expect God to bless you according to Proverbs 28:20: "A faithful man will be richly blessed...." With confidence lift your personal needs to God in prayer.

■ Make a list of the missionaries you support around the world. Remember, the ministry they provide is also being credited to your eternal account.

Thought for the Day:

"None of us has to be an accountant to know what 10 percent of a gross income is, but each of us has to be a person on his knees before God if we are to understand our commitment to proportionate giving. Proportionate to what? Proportionate to the accumulated wealth of one's family? Proportionate to one's income and the demands upon it, which vary from family to family? Proportionate to one's sense of security and the degree of anxiety with which one lives? Proportionate to the keenness of our awareness of those who suffer? Proportionate to our sense of justice and of God's ownership of all wealth? Proportionate to our sense of stewardship for those who follow after us? And so on, and so forth. The answer, of course, is in proportion to all of these things."[5]

— Elizabeth O'Connor

Scripture for the Day:

"One man gives freely, yet gains even more;
    another withholds unduly, but comes to poverty.
A generous man will prosper;
    he who refreshes others will himself be refreshed."

— Proverbs 11:24,25

"'Do not store up for yourselves treasures on earth, where moth and rust destroy, and where thieves break in and steal. But store up for yourselves treasures in heaven, where moth and rust do not destroy, and where thieves do not break in and steal. For where your treasure is, there your heart will be also.'"

— Matthew 6:19–21

A MAN AND THE CRISES LIFE BRINGS

" **I** have since learned that when a baffling or painful experience comes, the crucial thing is not always to find the right answers, but to ask the right questions. Self–questioning is a far more essential ingredient in life than I ever supposed. It's the water that keeps the modeling clay of our life from hardening into something forever rigid and unchanging. To refuse to ask honest questions of ourselves ultimately means shutting ourselves off from revelation. Often it is simply the right question at the right time that propels us on into the journey of awakening."[1]

— Sue Monk Kidd

CHAPTER 36

CHANGE AND LOSS

One Friday afternoon, shortly after we moved to Tulsa in 1980, I experienced an overwhelming feeling of loss, something I can only liken to grief. My throat got tight, I felt sad, and silent tears ran down my cheeks.

I felt stupid. This was a chance of a lifetime, the opportunity I had prayed and dreamed about, so why was I crying? I tried to reason with myself. Intellectually I was able to compute all of the advantages that my new position afforded, but it did nothing to change the way I felt. My sadness seemed immune to reason, and I began to seriously wonder if I had made a mistake in moving my family to Tulsa.

Only later did I learn that every major change in life is first experienced as a loss followed by a period of grief. I would never have thought that a promotion and a cross–country move would have anything in common with a divorce, unemployment, or even a death, but they do. Each one is a major change and is accompanied by a change in status, separation from friends and/or associates, and a period of grief. How long that grief lasts depends on how a person handles it. Repress it, and it will be around for a long time. Deal with it honestly, and you can speed up the adjustment and/or recovery period.

These many years later I now understand what was happening to me that Friday afternoon. I was grieving all I had left behind: the first home Brenda and I ever owned — the one we designed and built ourselves — a new church building, and a community where I was known and respected.

And these were minor losses compared to the friends I was leaving. No more Monday morning breakfasts at the Village Inn with Paul and Aileen. No more arty evenings and photo sessions with Jan and Susan. No more snowmobile outings with Darwin and Hazel. And no more picnics at Fish Creek Falls with Weldon and Elaine. No more! No more!

I was leaving everything I knew and loved, and everyone, with the exception of Brenda and Leah, who had played a major role in my life for the past five years. No wonder I was crying.

CHANGE AND LOSS

Nor is my experience unique. We are a mobile society. Jobs and career advancement make it necessary for us to move, often several times, especially during the early stages of our career. As a consequence, we are often separated from our roots, our family, and our childhood friends. This can be traumatic for the entire family, even the head of the house, as I discovered! How we deal with these emotions will not only determine how well we adjust to our new position, but also the quality of our relationships and family life, not to mention our confidence in God.

ACTION STEPS:
- List any major changes that you have experienced in the past year. Include things like your children's graduation or marriage, a move, a job change or promotion, unemployment, a major illness or surgery, a divorce, or the death of a family member or close friend.
- How have these changes affected your life? How do they make you feel? Angry? Sad? Helpless? Resentful? Have they affected the way you feel toward God? How are you dealing with these feelings and the changes that prompted them?
- Now surrender your experiences and the accompanying feelings to God and invite Him to redeem them, to bring something good out of them.

Thought for the Day:
"Every morning we read the Bible together, before our meditation. On the last day we had read the story of Lot's wife, who was turned into a pillar of salt because she looked back (Genesis 19:26). Then my friend exclaimed 'I am like Lot's wife. My life is petrified because I keep looking back. I turn that old problem over and over in my mind, uselessly, without ever discovering whether I did right or not. My life is no longer an adventure, because my faith is shaken and I am not looking for God's guidance any more. I want to start going forward again.' "[2]

— Paul Tournier

Scripture for the Day:
"And we know that in all things God works for the good of those who love him, who have been called according to his purpose."

— Romans 8:28

CHAPTER 37

UNEMPLOYED

T here was a time, not so long ago, when unemployment was something that only happened to the other guy. Not any more. Tough economic times, brought on by international competition and cheap overseas labor, have made job security a thing of the past. Men in my father's generation could expect to spend their entire careers with the same company systematically climbing the cooperate ladder. Today's worker, whether a blue–collar laborer or an executive, has little hope of that kind of security.

When a man suddenly finds himself unemployed, he experiences a host of emotions including a sense of alienation, a loss of self–esteem, and a feeling of powerlessness. Mark, an unemployed salesman, put it this way: "When my supervisor called me in and told me I was going to be let go because of the company's economic situation, I felt sick to my stomach. I felt as though my supervisor were saying, 'We don't need you anymore.'"[1]

If you've ever been laid off, you know what he's talking about. Yet, as tough as that feeling of rejection is, for many men the sense of powerlessness is worst. We are used to being in control, calling the shots. Now we realize that someone else has made a decision about our life, and there is nothing we can do about it. One morning we have a job, a position, that evening we don't. For years we've been the family breadwinner, and now we're unemployed, and powerless to rectify that situation.

Unemployment is traumatic, to be sure, but it does not have to be a disaster. When John was laid off, he struggled with depression initially but then decided to make the best of the situation. For a year or more he had talked of going back to school but he didn't see how he could afford it. Now he decided to use this time and his unemployment income as a means to further his education and better prepare himself for future employment. If he hadn't been laid off, he might never have pursued his dream of returning to school.

Being out of work can also force a man to examine his foundations, to ask himself some hard questions: Where do I get my value as a person: from my job or the amount of money I make? Where is my security, in God or in my job? When we are employed we usually ignore these questions or glibly answer them, and we are the poorer as a result. Faced with unemployment, we are forced to come to grips with these issues or risk plunging into despair or even a debilitating depression.

UNEMPLOYED

As men created in the image of God, we have value as persons simply because we are, not because of what we do or what we earn! Our work has nothing to do with our worth as persons. As Jesus said "'...a man's life does not consist in the abundance of his possessions.'"[2] Remember, God loves us whether we are working or not. Our friends and families love us even though we are unemployed. We are men of worth by virtue of the fact that we are children of God, nothing more.

And God will provide for us, the Scriptures promise that!

"'Do not set your heart on what you will eat or drink; do not worry about it. For the pagan world runs after all such things, and your Father knows that you need them. But seek his kingdom, and these things will be given to you as well.'"[3]

ACTION STEPS:

■ If you are unemployed, determine right now that you will not waste this time. Spend quality time with your family. Do the odd jobs around the house that you could never find time to do. Give your services to the church or another volunteer organization. Go back to school. You may never have this kind of time again, so don't waste it.

■ Unemployment can give us the courage to risk starting over in a new field. Since we spend much of our life working, we might as well do something we like, something we find meaningful. Ask yourself what you would really like to do with the rest of your life if money were no object. If you are serious, then get started.

■ Commit your vocational life to God and ask Him to direct your decisions.

Thought for the Day:

"God speaks to the crowd, but his call comes to individuals, and through their personal obedience he acts. He does not promise them nothing but success, or even final victory in this life....God does not promise that he will protect them from trials, from material cares, from sickness, from physical or moral suffering. He promises only that he will be with them in all these trials, and that he will sustain them if they remain faithful to him."[4]

— Paul Tournier

Scripture for the Day:

"I was young and now I am old,
    yet I have never seen the righteous forsaken
or their children begging bread."

— Psalm 37:25

CHAPTER 38

WHEN SICKNESS STRIKES

If you've never been seriously ill before, it may be difficult for you to cope with everything that is happening to you. First there is the pain, constant and unrelenting, as persistent as gravity, blotting out all else, until the world is no larger than your sick room. Then there's the weakness, the inability to control your own body, to make it function on command. Your body has become an enemy, undermining your morale, even your faith.

On a psychological level, you experience a loss of power, especially when you have to be hospitalized. Your familiar surroundings are gone. You find yourself in an environment in which you have little or no control. Before you became ill, you set your own schedule, within reasonable limits, of course. You decided when to get up and when to go to bed; what to eat, how to prepare it and when to eat it.

Suddenly all of that changes. You are placed in a hospital where you receive the finest medical care possible, but you no longer have control of your own life. You are told when to sleep, when to wake up, when to shower, and on some occasions you are even expected to relieve yourself on command. You are subjected to all kinds of humiliating procedures, stripped of all modesty, poked and prodded, and experimented upon — all in the name of medicine. Eventually all of this may produce healing, but initially it is demoralizing.

Then there's the fear. Fear of the unknown: What's going to happen to me? Will I get well? Will I still be able to provide for my family, care for my children?

Mundane concerns too: Will my insurance cover the hospital bills? Do I have enough sick leave? Will I still have a job when I get well?

Interlaced with all these are the questions raised by the ever-present possibility that you may not recover: Am I going to die? If so, what will become of my family? Who will look after the children?

On top of all of that, you may have a crisis of faith. Pain and suffering can make God seem distant and unconcerned, especially if it seems He isn't responding to your prayers. You may experience anger at your inability to rectify the situation. You will probably be tempted to take it out on the doctors and other health professionals, or you may direct it toward your spouse. Your rage is really directed toward the disease that threatens you, or toward God Who has "let" this happen to you, or even toward your own helplessness.

How you handle these volatile emotions will determine your rate of recovery and the quality of your life, not to mention the vibrancy of your faith. When you

WHEN SICKNESS STRIKES

are confronted with a serious illness, you really have just three choices. As pointed out by Arthur Gordon in *A Touch of Wonder*,[1] you can curse life for doing this to you, and look for some way to express your grief and rage. You can grit your teeth and endure it. Or you can accept it. As Gordon has noted, "the first alternative is useless. The second is sterile and exhausting. The third is the only way."[2]

Don't confuse acceptance with resignation. Resignation gives up and says, "Whatever will be will be." Acceptance, on the other hand, keeps believing for a miracle even as it accepts the reality of the illness. Acceptance does not demand a predetermined conclusion, rather it leaves the nature of the miracle to the wisdom of God. It may come in the form of divine healing, or it may come as a miracle in your spirit enabling you to experience God's peace even as you face an uncertain future.

And that's the real strength of Christianity. Not that it makes us immune to life's difficulties, but that it gives us resources to deal with them redemptively.

ACTION STEPS:

■ If you are facing a serious illness, or some other crisis in your life, ask God to help you get in touch with your feelings. Now honestly confess those feelings to God. It may be helpful to write out your confession. For example, you might write: "God, I feel cheated. All my life I've worked hard and lived a clean life and when I finally reached the place where I could begin to enjoy life, this hits me. It just doesn't seem fair. Don't You even care?"

■ When you have exhausted your feelings, surrender them to God one by one and ask Him to change the way you feel.

■ Make a conscious decision to trust God with your situation.

Thought for the Day:

"The sick reveal to us the existence of universal problems with which those who are well manage somehow to come to terms, without finding real solutions to them. I always think of the sick as a sort of magnifying–glass which shows up an anxiety which we all have within us, more or less unconsciously."[3]

— Paul Tournier

Scripture for the Day:

"...there was given me a thorn in my flesh, a messenger of Satan, to torment me. Three times I pleaded with the Lord to take it away from me. But he said to me, 'My grace is sufficient for you, for my power is made perfect in weakness.' Therefore I will boast all the more gladly about my weaknesses, so that Christ's power may rest on me."

— 2 Corinthians 12:7–9

CHAPTER 39

THE WISDOM OF GOD

omewhere we have picked up the idea that bad things don't happen to good people. That if we live a faithful and obedient life, we will be spared the pain and suffering that is so much a part of human experience. Such an idea, however, is neither Christian nor scriptural. In fact, any man who believes it is setting himself up for a devastating disappointment and quite possibly a crisis of faith.

Take the young couple who were expecting their first baby. They wanted everything to be perfect and prayed accordingly. They prayed that the baby would have perfect health, a gentle disposition, and a spiritual aptitude. According to their theology, this should have assured them of a perfect child. Imagine their bewilderment when their new–born daughter cried incessantly. In addition to the obvious concern they had for their baby, they were also tormented with self–doubt and questions regarding their faith. At the very time they most needed to be assured of God's love and faithfulness, their theology betrayed them.

Needless to say, all of this was more than they could bear. In desperation they came to see me. "Why," they demanded, "did God not answer our prayers? We prayed in faith. We did everything we were taught to do, so why didn't it work?" The answers I could have given them might have technically answered their questions, but they would not have resolved the real issue. Consequently, I chose to simply assure them of God's love and faithfulness. They were not satisfied.

A few weeks later the doctor discovered that their baby had a hernia, and surgery was scheduled. The appointed day arrived, and I went to the hospital to be with them. Long before I located the parents I could hear the baby wailing. Her anguished cries echoed forlornly down the long hospital corridors. Turning a final corner, I saw the young mother nervously pacing the hallway trying to comfort her baby, while her husband looked on helplessly.

THE WISDOM OF GOD

Approaching her I asked, "What seems to be the problem?"

"She's hungry," the distraught mother replied. "The doctor told us not to feed her after ten o'clock last night."

"Surely you're not going to let that stop you?" I asked with a straight face.

"What do you mean?" she asked, puzzled.

"I mean your baby's hungry and not to feed her is terribly cruel."

She looked at me like I had lost my mind. Finally she said, "It's dangerous for a person to have surgery on a full stomach, especially a baby."

Without giving her a chance to finish I interrupted. "Well, at least explain that to her. She must think you are a sadist. I mean, you carry her in your arms next to your breast, but you won't feed her. Even she knows you could if you wanted to, if you really cared."

"Don't be silly," she said with forced calmness, "you can't explain something like this to a three–month–old baby."

Gently I said, "I know what you are doing is an act of love. I know you have your baby's best interest at heart and so do you. But she doesn't understand that, and you're right, there's no way you can explain it to her."

Understanding began to brighten her tense features, so I continued, "That's the way it is with God. He is too wise to ever make a mistake, and too loving to ever cause one of His children needless pain. Still, He must sometimes risk our misunderstanding in order to do what's best for us. And we are simply too 'young,' too finite, to comprehend His infinite wisdom.

"Am I saying that God afflicted your baby daughter in order to develop character in your life, or to work out some other mysterious purpose? No! Not on your life. Did God allow it? Perhaps. For certain He will redeem it, that is, cause it to contribute to your ultimate good, but we may have to wait until eternity to see just how."

Like that young couple, you may be facing a crisis right now, and like them you may be asking why. You may even be tempted to rail at God about the apparent injustice of life, the unfairness of it all. Don't. That is just an exercise in futility. You must accept the fact that in this life we only "...see through a glass, darkly...[we only] know in part...."[1] Do that, and God will grant you a supernatural peace that is based on trust rather than understanding.

ACTION STEPS:

■ Make a choice right now to trust God even if you can't understand the "whys" of what you are going through. It is an act of your will through faith and it will enable you to stand firm regardless of how severe the storm may become.

■ Don't try to figure out how God is going to use this adversity for good. Trying to discover His ultimate purpose in such circumstances often leads to absurd conclusions or outright despair. Just trust Him.

Thought for the Day:

"Job, in the midst of undeserved suffering, shouts to God, barraging him with countless 'Whys?' The book ends without God ever having answered. Thus the problem of unjust suffering has remained unresolved all through these centuries, that is, in its form of a syllogism over which all logical minds stumble: either God is all–powerful and therefore unjust, or else he is just but not all–powerful. Job, however, received his answer — an altogether different kind. It was not an intellectual reply, but an experience of God, once he paid attention to the questions God was asking. The philosophical problem of unjust suffering remains unsolved, but Job's attitude completely altered because he met God: 'I had heard of thee by the hearing of the ear, but now my eye sees thee' (Job 42:5). As long as men remain in a strictly intellectual frame of mind, they will always brandish their problems as so many challenges to which no satisfactory answer has come."[2]

— Paul Tournier

THE WISDOM OF GOD

Scripture for the Day:

"'Though he slay me, yet will I hope in him....'"

— Job 13:15

"'So keep up your courage, men, for I have faith in God that it will happen just as he told me.'"

— Acts 27:25

CHAPTER 40

MID–LIFE CRISIS

For several years we heard a lot about men and mid–life crisis, but that fascination now seems to have passed. The reality of mid–life, and the unique pressures it places on the male psyche, however, are still just as real. According to H. Norman Wright, "Midlife is the time when men discover that work, wealth, fame, status, exercise, health fads and diets have all been in vain in a sense, for they cannot prevent old age, illness or death. They do not stop the wheel of time from turning. Men see their parents lowered into the grave of death, feel their own body changes and see younger people moving ahead of them and taking over. And they ask themselves, 'Why?' "[1]

Another complicating factor is role reversal. A number of studies suggest that at mid–life men tend to move toward passivity, tenderness, and intimacy, which they previously repressed. Women, on the other hand, tend to become more autonomous, aggressive, and cognitive. It's not hard to see what this can do to a marriage. Just when he is turning toward her in search of intimacy, she is venturing out in search of autonomy. They are like ships passing in the night.

Many men feel trapped, everyone wants a piece of them. "I feel like a vending machine," Jim Conway writes, describing his own mid–life crisis in the midst of a successful pastorate. "Someone pushes a button, and out comes a sermon. Someone pushes another button, and out comes a magazine article. The family pushes buttons, and out comes dollars or time involvement. The community pushes other buttons, and I show up for meetings, sign petitions, and take stands."[2]

H. Norman Wright suggests that for other men mid–life becomes a war zone with numerous enemies. "One such enemy is his body. It no longer responds as it used to for it is slower and perhaps sagging. His body doesn't look as good nor does it have the stamina and energy it once did."[3]

A second enemy is work. He may have a prestigious position but he feels there has to be something more fulfilling than this. Or maybe he is on a treadmill to nowhere in his position. Either way he feels trapped, bored, and in financial bondage.

Strange as it may seem, a third enemy is his family. Again he has the feeling of entrapment. If it weren't for the financial obligations to the family, he could quit his job. He thinks about living off the land, or traveling. But the pressure of braces for teeth, tuitions for Christian schools, the mortgage and other financial demands from his wife and children press upon him.

MID–LIFE CRISIS

A fourth enemy is God. He is viewed as unfair and is blamed for the bind in which the man finds himself.[4] As the wise man wrote long ago, "A man's own folly ruins his life, yet his heart rages against the Lord."[5]

As Christian men we are not immune to the storms of mid–life, but neither do we have to succumb to them. While other men are making rash decisions and doing crazy things like having an affair with a younger woman, we can draw upon the resources of the Spirit and the Church to meet the challenges of mid–life. Indeed, mid–life can be an enriching time for the man who has prepared himself for it.

ACTION STEPS:

- If you are between the ages of thirty–five and fifty–five take an emotional inventory of your life. Do you feel trapped, used, unfulfilled, overwhelmed, or some similar emotion? Take a few minutes and write out a detailed description of your feelings.

- Now process these feelings with someone you trust — your wife, your pastor, or a male friend. The experience of sharing your feelings often makes them less overwhelming and more manageable. Pray about these issues together.

Thought for the Day:
All men experience some type of mid–life transition. Not all experience a crisis.
Many mid–life crises can be avoided by changing the cause.
Men can survive the mid–life crisis and move ahead in a positive way.[6]

— H. Norman Wright

Scripture for the Day:
"'They will build houses and dwell in them;
they will plant vineyards and eat their fruit.
No longer will they build houses and others live in them,
or plant and others eat.
For as the days of a tree,
so will be the days of my people;
my chosen ones will long enjoy
the works of their hands.
They will not toil in vain
or bear children doomed to misfortune;
for they will be a people blessed by the Lord,
they and their descendants with them.'"

— Isaiah 65:21–23

CHAPTER 41

PREVENTING A MID–LIFE CRISIS

While mid–life is inevitable, a mid–life crisis is not. Mid–life is a time of transition, a time when a man reevaluates his life goals and sets the course for his future. Not infrequently, he finds himself questioning his own value, his identity as a person and a man. It is this identity crisis which often precipitates his mid–life crisis.

In *Seasons of a Marriage*, H. Norman Wright says, "The answer to the identity crisis is fourfold: 1) Build an adequate identity upon a solid base; 2) Become more complete in our humanity by experiencing and expressing feelings; 3) Develop strong friendships with other men; 4) Prepare for life crisis and changes by incorporating God's Word into our lives."[1]

The key is what Gail Sheehy calls "concomitant growth" which is a term used to describe the need to develop concurrently on the three or four basic frontiers of our life. These frontiers include: our work, our relationships with significant others, our own unique selfhood, and our relationship with God.

Unfortunately, we tend to overinvest in our career at the expense of all the other areas of our lives, especially in our early years. The effects of this imbalance begin to surface sometime in our middle years. By this time we are often "successful" but unfulfilled. Or we suddenly come face to face with the fact that, for all of our hard work, we have not attained the status in life to which we aspired. As a result we are assailed with self–doubt and questions about our value as men, which often results in the infamous "mid–life crisis." The time to prevent a crisis is now, and the place to start is with our identity. We are not just what we do, i.e., a computer programmer, or a carpenter, or a salesman. We are men created in the image of God; sons of God both by creation and by adoption. And as men made in the image of God, we function in many roles: husband, father, breadwinner, spiritual leader, friend, etc. Should we experience failure or disappointment in one of our roles, we do not experience a crisis, because our value as men is not dependent exclusively on that one role.

We must also learn to be more expressive. I realize that this goes against the grain. Most of us have been taught that men don't cry. We have been encouraged to deny our feelings rather than express them. Unfortunately, repression is not a healthy way to deal with our emotions, and as a result many men experience a crisis of emotion sometime in their middle years.

Learning to express our feelings may require a supreme effort. Many of us will have to unlearn years of training. We will have to develop a whole new vocabulary of "feeling" words. And we will have to build the kind of intimate relationships in which it is safe to share our feelings. The resulting richness of our lives, however, is well worth the effort.

This commitment to become expressive leads naturally into the area of friendship. We must not share our deepest feelings indiscriminately, rather we must cultivate friendships with other men, a trust relationship in which we can share our hearts without fear of rejection or ridicule.

Once again we find ourselves swimming upstream. Intimate friendships have been the special domain of women. Women talk to each other. Men do things together. In order to fully experience our potential as men created in the image of God, we must break through this relational barrier and develop transparent relationships with other men. Friendships in which we can be open and honest with one another.

The fourth step in preventing a mid–life crisis is to incorporate God's Word into our lives. The Scriptures enable us to interpret life from God's eternal perspective rather than from our limited understanding. Even if the circumstances of life conspire to make us feel insignificant, we know that "the Spirit himself testifies with our spirit that we are God's children. Now if we are children, then we are heirs — heirs of God and co–heirs with Christ....our present sufferings are not worth comparing with the glory that will be revealed in us."[2]

ACTION STEPS:

- It's time to ask yourself some hard questions:

    1) What is the primary source of my identity?

    2) How do I handle my feelings? Do I find appropriate ways to share them or do I repress them?

    3) Who is my best friend? Do I share honestly and deeply with him? Is our friendship built around activities or shared experiences?

    4) Is the Word of God a vital part of my life? In what way?

- List the steps you are going to take in order to prevent a mid–life crisis in your life.

Thought for the Day:

"Preoccupation with self is a weakness in adolescents, [but] it becomes an essential task in adulthood, for developing a coherent view of life and coming to terms with the uniqueness of one's individuality are so important."[3]

— John Claypool

Scripture for the Day:

"Trust in the Lord with all your heart and lean not on your own understanding; in all your ways acknowledge him, and he will make your paths straight."

— Proverbs 3:5,6

CHAPTER 42

FACING DEATH

I t is a sobering moment when you realize, for the first time, that your parents aren't going to live forever. Theoretically you have always known that, but it really hits home during mid–life. It happened to me in 1985 when my seemingly indestructible father was stricken with heart disease.

Dad underwent two major surgeries in the space of three weeks. The first was double by–pass open–heart surgery, and then three weeks later he had his gall bladder removed. I wasn't able to get a flight in time to be there before Dad went into surgery the second time. In fact, it was well past ten o'clock that night when I finally made it to the hospital. Dad acknowledged my presence, but that was about all he could manage before succumbing to the pain medication. About midnight I left Mother to her bedside vigil and drove "home" to the house where I grew up.

Opening the trunk to get my bag, I saw Dad's toolbox and his coveralls — symbols of his strength and resourcefulness. There wasn't anything he couldn't fix. In the living room I encountered his favorite chair, a lazy–boy recliner covered in a wool plaid. Now, it became a haunting symbol of his sickness. How many nights had he spent here, unable to sleep, alone with the darkness and his pain?

A deep sadness settled over me. I tried to reason it away. I was tired and lonely, the house was empty. My sadness wasn't fooled. I was face to face with my own mortality and Dad's.

I was tired but I couldn't sleep so I wandered through the empty house listening to the stillness. How different from my childhood when four kids created a constant commotion. How different from other trips home, holidays and vacations when the house rang with laughter, love, and grandchildren were everywhere underfoot. I sat in Dad's favorite chair and cried. I couldn't help it.

Yet even in my sadness, I realized that there was much to be thankful for. Dad and I had shared on a deeper level than we had known before. We didn't want a single affirming word left unshared, any feeling of love unexpressed. I remembered holding his hand the day before his open–heart surgery and the closeness we felt. The way he blinked to hold back his tears when he told me all the things he had wanted to do for Mother and hadn't got to, at least not yet. Some improvements on the house and a trip to Hawaii. After awhile, he fell asleep and I was left with my thoughts and the realization of how much I loved that special man I call Dad.

This reliving of the past went on all night long as I tossed fitfully, unable to sleep, with only God and my memories to keep me company. Along about dawn, I

FACING DEATH

realized that even if Dad died, he would live on in the memories we had made. The thirty–eight years we had shared had enough love and laughter for two or three lifetimes. No one could ever take Dad's place, I understood that better than ever now, but I would always have the memories and the God he made more real to me than life.

Thankfully, Dad recovered from his surgeries and is still alive today. But as a result of that painful experience I now know better how to prepare for the inevitable moment we must all face. When Dad finally goes the way of all flesh, I will not grieve over what might have been, rather I will thank God for what we had. Dad would want it that way.

That doesn't mean I won't grieve, or that I won't miss him. It just means that even our sorrow can be a source of spiritual richness if we have an unshakable faith and a lifetime of shared experiences to draw upon.

ACTION STEPS:
■ Examine your relationship with your parents. Do you have any unfinished business with them, any unresolved issues? If so, determine a time when you will come to closure with them on these issues. Now seek the counsel and prayers of your pastor or a wise Christian brother concerning the best way to handle everything.

■ Write a letter reminiscing about some of your favorite childhood memories. Express your love and thankfulness to your parents for their influence in your life.

■ Plan a special family gathering to honor your parents.

Thought for the Day:
"At this point in life or in the near future you may experience the death of a parent, a close friend or your spouse. You may even face the prospect of your own dying....You cannot run from the death of another nor from your own death. You need to consider in advance what you will experience when you know you are dying. This will help you be better able to handle your inner turmoil and reactions. And if someone close to you is dying, knowing what he or she will experience will make you more able to minister."[1]

— H. Norman Wright

Scripture for the Day:
"I have fought the good fight, I have finished the race, I have kept the faith. Now there is in store for me the crown of righteousness, which the Lord, the righteous Judge, will award to me on that day — and not only to me, but also to all who have longed for his appearing."

— 2 Timothy 4:7,8

A MAN AND HIS DECISIONS

"God guides us, despite our uncertainties and our vagueness, even through our failings and mistakes....He leads us step by step, from event to event. Only afterwards, as we look back over the way we have come and reconsider certain important moments in our lives in the light of all that has followed them, or when we survey the whole progress of our lives, do we experience the feeling of having been led without knowing it, the feeling that God has mysteriously guided us."[1]

— Paul Tournier

CHAPTER 43

FINDING GOD'S WILL

inding the will of God is often difficult for even the most spiritually mature. It's not always easy to discern between God's voice and our own. For instance, the Apostle Paul and his companions made three attempts to determine God's direction for their ministry before they got it right. They tried to preach the Word in the province of Asia and were stopped by the Holy Spirit. Next they attempted to enter Bithynia, but once more the Spirit prevented them. "So they passed by Mysia and went down to Troas. During the night Paul had a vision of a man of Macedonia standing and begging him, 'Come over to Macedonia and help us.' After Paul had seen the vision," Luke says, "we got ready at once to leave for Macedonia, concluding that God had called us to preach the gospel to them."[2]

That's encouraging, at least it is to me. If a spiritual giant like Paul struggled to discern the will of God, then maybe there's some hope for us. I mean, if God gave Paul three chances to get it right, then surely He won't give up on us. In truth, God is far more determined to make His will known to us than we are to know it.

While God made His will known to Paul through a vision (or a dream), it has been my experience that He usually speaks to us in more ordinary ways. Take David Wilkerson, for example. In 1958 he was the pastor of a comfortable church in Philipsburg, Pennsylvania, when God spoke to him in a way that would shape his ministry for the rest of his life. It started while he was reading the *Life* magazine account of seven teenagers who were on trial for the murder of a fifteen–year–old polio victim named Michael Farmer. For days afterwards he was haunted by their youthful faces, desperate and angry. Escape was impossible, no matter what he was doing they were never far from his mind. Even in prayer they were before him, and intercession only amplified his concern. Finally, he surrendered and drove to New York City.

Once there, he was at a loss as how to proceed. In desperation he decided to approach Judge Davidson, who was presiding over the trial. Perhaps he would grant him permission to visit the accused in jail. There had been several threats against the judge's life, and security was tight. Still, David managed to approach him as he was leaving the courtroom and promptly got himself arrested. He was finally released after he convinced the authorities that he was a preacher and not some kind of assassin.

When he emerged from the courtroom a group of reporters were waiting for him. They immediately surrounded him and began firing questions. Several flashbulbs popped, and David suddenly saw it all: "Bible–waving preacher interrupts the Michael Farmer murder trial."

And he was right, his worst fears were realized. Not only did the New York papers run the story, but the United Press syndicate account was also picked up by several smaller papers. By the time he arrived back in Philipsburg, the whole town was buzzing, his telephone was ringing off the wall, and none of the calls was complimentary. He felt like a fool. It seemed as if he had embarrassed, not only himself, but also his church, and perhaps even God.

For several days he buried himself in his work and tried to forget the whole humiliating episode, but it was no use. That *Life* magazine article had become his Macedonian vision. He was literally driven to return to New York City. God simply would not give him any rest.

Once he was back in the city, everything began to fall into place. He parked his car and started walking. Before he covered the first block someone called, "Hey Davie, preacher." Turning, he saw half a dozen teenage gang members approaching.

A MAN AND HIS DECISIONS

"Aren't you the preacher that got kicked out of the Michael Farmer trial?" one of them asked. "I saw your picture in the paper. I'd know your face anywhere."

"He's one of us," the leader said. "The cops don't like him and they don't like us."

That incident was David Wilkerson's *carte blanche* with the street gangs of New York City, and the rest is history. Subsequently, he founded Teen Challenge International, the most successful drug rehabilitation program in the world. With John and Elizabeth Sherril he wrote *The Cross and the Switchblade*, the account of his work with the street gangs in New York City, which became an international best-seller and a vital part of the Charismatic Renewal. The book was later made into a major motion picture starring Pat Boone.

As a result of his personal experience, David Wilkerson says, "The will of God grows on you. That which is of God will fasten itself on you and overpower and possess your entire being. That which is not of God will die — you will lose interest. But the plan of God will never die. The thing God wants you to do will become stronger each day in your thoughts, in your prayers, in your planning. It grows and grows!"[3]

FINDING GOD'S WILL

ACTION STEPS:

■ Ask yourself these questions: Is God trying to speak to me through my desires? If so, what is He trying to say to me?

■ Have I been obedient to these inner urges of the Spirit? If not, what keeps me from doing so?

Thought for the Day:

"The way in which the Holy Spirit, therefore, usually works, in a fully obedient soul, in regard to this direct guidance, is to impress upon the mind a wish or desire to do or to leave undone certain things."[4]

— Hannah Whitall Smith

Scripture for the Day:

"And now, compelled by the Spirit, I am going to Jerusalem, not knowing what will happen to me there. I only know that in every city the Holy Spirit warns me that prison and hardships are facing me. However, I consider my life worth nothing to me, if only I may finish the race and complete the task the Lord Jesus has given me — the task of testifying to the gospel of God's grace."

— Acts 20:22–24

SURRENDERED DESIRES

The first step in discerning the will of God is unconditional surrender. Many of us pray, "God show me Your will," so we can decide whether we want to do it or not. But God doesn't make His will known simply to satisfy our curiosity. It is revealed most frequently as marching orders to the committed, to the one who has prayed, "I'll go where You want me to go, I'll do what You want me to do."

God usually speaks to me through my belly; that is, I have a sense when something is right, when it's God's will. It's a "gut feeling," and over the years I've learned to trust it. Inevitably someone wants me to be more specific. "What exactly," they ask, "do you mean by a 'gut feeling?'" When pressed, I define it as my surrendered desires.

Here's how it works. I bring all of my hopes and dreams, all of my ambitions and desires, and lay them at the foot of the cross. I give them to God, praying, "Lord Jesus, I give You permission to change my desires, to superimpose Your will on mine. Now guide me through my desires." Then I do what I want to do, believing that my desires now reflect God's direction for my life.

While I trust these inner promptings, I do not accept them as infallible. In fact, I submit them to three tests. First, the Word test: Is this desire scriptural? Second, the time test: Now that I've waited a while has the intensity of my desire grown or waned? And third, the door test: Has God opened a door of opportunity so I can pursue my desire?

If it fails any of these tests, then I discard it and continue no further. Remember, God's will can stand the test of time and scrutiny, so don't be afraid to test His guidance. It is not doubt, but wisdom which motivates us to test the spirit.

SURRENDERED DESIRES

ACTION STEPS:
- Take a moment right now and surrender all of your hopes and dreams, all of your thoughts and desires, to Jesus Christ. Invite Him to transform your desires until they reflect His will for your life.
- Since it is human nature to be self–centered, I have discovered that I must surrender my will to God anew every day. Determine right now to make surrender a part of your daily walk.
- List any specific steps you are now going to take in order to live out the will of God in your life.

Thought for the Day:
"There are four ways in which He reveals His will to us —through the Scriptures, through providential circumstances, through the convictions of our own higher judgment, and through the inward impressions of the Holy Spirit on our minds."[1]

— Hannah Whitall Smith

Scripture for the Day:
"But the Lord said to me,'....You must go to everyone I send you to and say whatever I command you. Do not be afraid of them, for I am with you and will rescue you,' declares the Lord."

— Jeremiah 1:7,8

CHAPTER 45

TESTING THE WILL OF GOD

od most often guides us through our surrendered desires. Which is to say that once we surrender unconditionally we usually receive a sense of direction, some inner prompting, a sanctified desire. While I believe that these desires generally express God's will, I still must submit them to the Word test. I ask myself: What does the Scripture say about this desire? Is it prohibited by direct command or scriptural principle? Remember, God's special guidance will never violate His revealed will, which is expressed in the Word.

One Sunday morning at the conclusion of worship I was approached by a young woman who desired prayer. She told me that she was engaged to be married, but as the wedding drew near she was experiencing some troubling second thoughts. As a committed believer she was concerned about marrying an unsaved man and wanted me to pray with her for guidance. I gently refused, reasoning that there was nothing to pray about. God's will was already revealed in His word. "Do not be yoked together with unbelievers. For what do righteousness and wickedness have in common? Or what fellowship can light have with darkness?....What does a believer have in common with an unbeliever?"[1]

The late A. W. Tozer put it so clearly when he said that we should never seek guidance about what God has already forbidden. Nor should we ever seek guidance in the areas where God has already said yes and given us a command. In those instances, what we need is not guidance but obedience.

If my desire passes the Word test, then I submit it to the time test. If a desire is really divine direction, then the longer I delay, the stronger it becomes. As Jeremiah said, "...his word is in my heart like a burning fire, shut up in my bones...."[2] On the other hand, if it is just a personal whim and I wait, surrendered, submitting it to the time test, it will fade away.

Finally, if it's compatible with the Word, and if it passes the time test, then I submit it to the door test. Keith Miller says, "This is sort of like rattling door handles to see if you can find a door which is unlocked...."[3]

More than twelve years ago I had an experience that illustrates this principle perfectly. For almost five and a half years I had served as pastor of the Church of the Comforter in Craig, Colorado. They were some of the best years of my life. While there, I wrote two books, built a new house, and led the church through a successful building program. Yet, after five years I was feeling restless. The new facilities were finished, and the congregation seemed ready to launch new ministries into the community, but my heart wasn't in it.

After the restlessness had persisted for several weeks I prayed: "God, I don't trust my emotions. I feel like it is time for me to make a move, yet I can't be sure. If this restlessness comes from You, if it's time for me to change churches, then You will have to open the door."

Within two weeks I received a telephone call from Christian Chapel in Tulsa, Oklahoma. In my fifteen years of ministry I had never preached in Oklahoma, and no one in Tulsa had ever heard of Richard Exley. Still, through a series of divinely directed events, I came to the attention of the pulpit committee, and they invited me to interview for the position of senior pastor.

When the congregation extended the call, my wife and I accepted and moved to Tulsa. Things weren't easy; they seldom are. Our house in Colorado didn't sell for a year, Brenda was forced to work outside the home in order to make ends meet, and our daughter Leah had trouble adjusting to her new school; yet in it all we had a sense of security. Beneath all the surface storms we had an underlying calm — the confidence that comes from being obedient, from being in the center of God's perfect will.

Now, twelve years later, I am more convinced than ever that it was God's guidance that brought us to Christian Chapel. It began with a restlessness that wouldn't go away; then God sovereignly opened the door, and the rest, as they say, is history.

Remember, God has a plan for your life, and He wants to make it known to you. There are risks, to be sure. You may misunderstand and do the wrong thing, but He is able to take even your unintentional mistakes and make them contribute to your ultimate growth. "The Lord will fulfill his purpose for [you]...."[4]

ACTION STEPS:

■ In order to test your desires against the Scriptures, you will have to know them. Find a Bible–reading schedule that will enable you to read the Scriptures through in one year, and get started.

■ If possible, find a friend who will agree to read the Bible through with you. Make an agreement to hold each other accountable.

■ Schedule a time each week when you and your friend can get together and discuss the things you are discovering in the Scriptures. Talk specifically about the ways God's eternal truth speaks directly to your life.

TESTING THE WILL OF GOD

Thought for the Day:

"Maintain at all costs a daily time of Scripture reading and prayer. As I look back, I see that the most formative influence in my life and thought has been my daily contact with Scripture over 60 years."[5]

— Frank Gaebelein

Scripture for the Day:

"I rejoice in following your statutes

as one rejoices in great riches.

I meditate on your precepts

and consider your ways.

I delight in your decrees;

I will not neglect your word."

— Psalm 119:14–16

CHAPTER 46

ONE STEP AT A TIME

hen God told Abraham to leave his country, his people, and his father's household, did He speak in an audible voice, one that Abraham could hear with his natural ear? I don't know, and neither does anyone else, at least not for certain. Most of us, I think, tend to assume that He did. Somehow it makes Abraham's obedience easier to accept, and by the same token, it makes our own indecision less reproachful. I mean, if God would speak to us in an audible voice, wouldn't it be easier for us to obey?

Unfortunately, God doesn't very often speak that way, or even through dreams, visions, or visitations. He does on occasion, but it's the exception rather than the rule. Usually His instructions come as an inner witness, what the Scriptures call a "still small voice."[1] What is it Joan of Arc says in Shaw's play when someone tells her that the voices she hears are not God, but her imagination? "Of course," she replies, "that is how the messages of God come to us."[2]

And so it is. Still, whatever form divine guidance takes there is always the risk of human error. We do the very best we can to discern the will of God, but in the end there are no guarantees. Maybe that's what the Scriptures mean when they say, "We walk by faith, not by sight."[3] A man has to act on what he feels is God's direction, even though there is no way that he can be absolutely sure that the voice he is following is God's voice and not his own.

Even when we are reasonably sure that God has spoken, we still don't have the complete picture. Take Abraham, for instance. He "...obeyed and went, even though he did not know where he was going."[4] All Abraham really knew was that he was driven to separate himself from his father's family, and his father's country, and he identified that inner compulsion as the voice of God.

ONE STEP AT A TIME

If we wait until we have resolved every doubt, every question, before following God we will never do anything with our life. We must step out by faith; we must go and do whatever it is we think God is calling us to do. Being assured, as Paul Tournier says, that, "God guides us, despite our uncertainties and our vagueness, even through our failings and mistakes."[5]

It helps me to think of guidance as a miner's cap with its built-in lamp whose feeble beam penetrates the darkness only a step or two. As the miner steps out, the light penetrates ever deeper, one step at a time. So it is with God's guidance. We receive further direction only as we walk in the light He has already given us.

ACTION STEPS:

■ Look back at some of the major decisions you have made and see if you can identify some things, which at first glace, appeared to be coincidences, but on closer examination you now realize were God's doing.

■ As you examine your life, see if you can identify specific patterns; that is, ways in which God has revealed or worked out His purpose for your life.

■ Now see if you can identify any of those patterns that are at work in your life right now. If so, list them and ask God to enable you to understand what they mean so you can work with Him to accomplish His purposes in your life.

Thought for the Day:

"...His suggestions will come to us, not so much commands from the outside as desires springing up within. They will originate in our will; we shall feel as though we *desired* to do so and so, not as though we *must*."[6]

— Hannah Whitall Smith

Scripture for the Day:

"The steps of a good man are ordered by the Lord: and he delighteth in his way. Though he fall, he shall not be utterly cast down: for the Lord upholdeth him with his hand."

— Psalm 37:23,24 KJV

A MAN AND TEMPTATION

"For there is only one sin, and it is characteristic of the whole world. It is the self–will which prefers 'my' way to God's — which puts 'me' in the centre where only God is in place."[1]

— William Temple

CHAPTER 47

TEMPTATION IS NOT A SIN

f you are like most men who are striving to live a godly life, you feel guilty when you are tempted. Somehow we think that if we were the kind of Christian we should be that we would be immune to temptation. At least we would be immune to the kind of base temptations that accost us. Now that's a noble thought, but it's just not true. Spiritual maturity enables us to more effectively resist temptation, but it does not make us immune to it.

Consider the example of Jesus. He was the most spiritually whole person the world has ever known, and yet He was "...tempted in every way, just as we are...."[2] If Jesus was not immune to temptation, then how can we possibly think that we will be? Are we more spiritually mature, more holy, than He was? Hardly.

Another reason we feel guilty when we are tempted is because we are unable to clearly distinguish where temptation ends and sin begins. Knowing this, the enemy does everything within his power to confuse us at this point. And if we rely only on our emotions he will undoubtedly succeed, because when we are tempted we "feel" sinful.

In times of temptation, then, we must turn to the Scriptures. The eternal Word will resolve any questions we have about temptation and sin. Probably the best place to start is with Jesus Himself. As we have seen, the Bible tells us that He was "...tempted in every way, just as we are — yet was without sin."[3] From this passage, and countless others, we must conclude that temptation is not a sin — regardless of how it makes us feel. A clear understanding at this point will free us from the kind of lingering guilt that makes us vulnerable to the exploitation of the enemy.

Finally, we must learn to use the Word of God to resist temptation. In this, as in all things, Jesus is our example. Each time He was tempted, He used the Scriptures to defend Himself. When He was tempted to turn stones into bread, He said, " 'It is written: "Man does not live on bread alone." ' "[4] When Satan promised Him the splendor and authority of all the world's kingdoms if He would fall down and worship him, Jesus replied, " 'It is written: "Worship the Lord your

TEMPTATION IS NOT A SIN

God and serve him only." ' "⁵ And when Satan challenged Him to prove that He was the Son of God by leaping from the pinnacle of the temple, Jesus again answered, " 'It says: "Do not put the Lord your God to the test." ' "⁶

Temptation is inevitable, a fact of life in our fallen world. We cannot avoid it, but we can overcome it. God has made provision for our victory, "...[He] is faithful; he will not let you be tempted beyond what you can bear. But when you are tempted, he will also provide a way out so that you can stand up under it."⁷

ACTION STEPS:

■ Develop the habit of clearly distinguishing between temptation, which is a desire, and sin, which is an act.

■ If you are repeatedly tempted in the same areas (i.e., lust, anger, greed, etc.), examine your daily life and habits to see what behaviors make you susceptible to these temptations. Now ask God to help you modify your behavior accordingly.

■ List some of the changes you are going to make in your daily life to minimize temptation.

Thought for the Day:

"You have gone through the big crisis, now be alert over the least things....You have remained true to God under great and intense trials, now beware of the undercurrent. Do not be morbidly introspective, looking forward with dread, but keep alert; keep your memory bright before God. Unguarded strength is double weakness because that is where the 'retired sphere of the leasts' saps. The Bible characters fell on their strong points, never on their weak ones."⁸

— Oswald Chambers

Scripture for the Day:

"Because he [Jesus] himself suffered when he was tempted, he is able to help those who are being tempted."

— Hebrews 2:18

"I have hidden your word in my heart that I might not sin against you."

— Psalm 119:11

CHAPTER 48

WHEN LUST IS CONCEIVED

Some years ago a man came to my office for counseling. He chose to see me rather than his own pastor, so great was his shame. He had done a despicable thing, and now he couldn't live with himself. Hardly had I closed the office door before he fell to his knees sobbing. For several minutes he wept before the Lord. Finally he was able to compose himself and only then did he share his dark secret.

He was a good man, a Christian, and he never intended to become involved in sin, but he had. It had started innocently enough with morning coffee at a nearby convenience store. Then he began browsing through the pornographic magazines displayed on the counter. A couple of days later he purchased one, then another.

From that point, his story follows an all too familiar progression. From magazines he went to x–rated videos, and then he secured the services of a prostitute. Of course, this degenerating sequence didn't happen overnight. It took place over a period of months and with each step he told himself he would go no farther, but he seemed powerless to stop.

He lived in a self–made hell. There were moments of lustful pleasure, to be sure, but they were followed by hours of shame, days and weeks of unspeakable regret. Yet even in his shame he was irresistibly drawn toward the very thing he hated. His desperate prayers seemed powerless against the demons within.

Secrecy and fear became a way of life. What if someone saw him? What if his wife found out or someone from his church? His marriage suffered as did his church life. He wanted out, he wanted to stop, but something seemed to drive him on.

Then his worst fears were realized. He contacted a sexually transmitted disease and infected his wife. Thankfully it wasn't AIDS, but it still meant that he had to tell her so she could receive treatment. What was going to happen now? Would she forgive him? Could she ever trust him again? How foolish, how insane, his sins now seemed.

After hearing his confession, I helped him identify his failures and the steps necessary to rectify them. He had failed God, sinned against Him, and now he needed forgiveness and restoration. He had failed his wife, been unfaithful to her, broken their wedding vows, and now he had to acknowledge his sins against their marriage and seek her forgiveness as well. And he had sinned against himself,

WHEN LUST IS CONCEIVED

betrayed his own values, dishonored everything he had once held sacred and dear.

We prayed together then, claiming 1 John 1:9, "If we confess our sins, he is faithful and just and will forgive us our sins and purify us from all unrighteousness." God's forgiveness was wonderful beyond words, but how much better it would have been if he had simply resisted temptation.

Together we began to plot a scriptural strategy for dealing with future temptation. There were certain things he couldn't do, certain places he couldn't go, not because they were sinful in themselves, but because of his propensity to sin. For instance, he could not go into a convenience store, the risk was simply too great. Nor could he go into any place that rented videos. Extreme? Perhaps, but we were dealing with matters of life and death: "'If your right eye causes you to sin, gouge it out and throw it away. It is better for you to lose one part of your body than for your whole body to be thrown into hell.'"[1]

That was many years ago, and I'm thankful I can tell you that God's grace was sufficient for that man and for his wife. The road back was painful beyond words, requiring months of marital counseling and intense personal ministry, but it was well worth it. Today they are happily married and active in their church.

ACTION STEPS:

■ What can you learn from this man's painful experience? Make a list of the things and carry them with you in your briefcase or wallet.

■ If there are areas in your life where you are courting temptation, identify them and take immediate steps to rectify them.

■ Confess your temptations to a trusted friend or to your pastor and ask him to hold you accountable.

Thought for the Day:

"The only time to stop temptation is at the first point of recognition. If one begins to argue and engage in a hand to hand combat, temptation almost always wins the day."[2]

— Thomas a Kempis

Scripture for the Day:

"When tempted, no one should say, 'God is tempting me.' For God cannot be tempted by evil, nor does he tempt anyone; but each one is tempted when, by his own evil desire, he is dragged away and enticed. Then, after desire has conceived, it gives birth to sin; and sin, when it is full-grown, gives birth to death."

— James 1:13–15

CHAPTER 49

FAILURE IS PROGRESSIVE

In the previous chapter I shared the tragic story of a Christian man who found himself in bondage to pornography and illicit sex after succumbing to a series of small temptations. While his experience may be more sensational than most, it is a classic example of the way temptation works.

This same pattern is readily apparent in Peter's life. He denied Jesus three times and with a curse, yet his denial was not an isolated incident. It was preceded by at least five small failures which set the stage.

First, there was his overconfidence. On the night that Jesus was betrayed He told Peter: "'...today — yes, tonight — before the rooster crows twice you yourself will disown me three times.'"[1] Instead of admitting his vulnerability and seeking help while there was still time, "...Peter insisted emphatically, 'Even if I have to die with you, I will never disown you'...."[2]

The second step was prayerlessness. When Peter went with Jesus into Gethsemane later that same night, he slept rather than praying, prompting Jesus to chide him, " 'Why are you sleeping?...Get up and pray so that you will not fall into temptation.' "[3]

Next he succumbed to misguided zeal. When Judas and a detachment of soldiers came to arrest Jesus, Peter drew his sword and struck the high priest's servant, cutting off his right ear. Then Jesus rebuked him, "...'Put your sword away! Shall I not drink the cup the Father has given me?'"[4]

Step four was distancing and step five was fellowship with the world. "Peter followed him [Jesus] at a distance, right into the courtyard of the high priest. There he sat with the guards and warmed himself at the fire."[5]

It wasn't long until a servant girl accused him of being a follower of Jesus, which he vehemently denied. "A little later someone else saw him and said, 'You also are one of them.'

"'Man, I am not!' Peter replied.

"About an hour later another asserted, 'Certainly this fellow was with him, for he is a Galilean.'

FAILURE IS PROGRESSIVE

"Peter replied, 'Man, I don't know what you're talking about!' Just as he was speaking, the rooster crowed. The Lord turned and looked straight at Peter. Then Peter remembered the word the Lord had spoken to him: 'Before the rooster crows today, you will disown me three times.'"[6]

At any point Peter might have repented and spared himself this final disgrace, but now it is too late. In the space of a single hour he denied Jesus three times. "And he went outside and wept bitterly."[7]

Is there a lesson here for us? I think so. As Thomas a Kempis pointed out in the *Imitation of Christ*, the only time to stop temptation is the moment it rears its ugly head. If one delays dealing with it, temptation almost always wins the day.

ACTION STEPS:

- As painful as it may be, recall a sinful failure. See if you can identify the earliest moment of temptation. It was probably some small thing, seemingly insignificant, hardly noticed. Now identify the successive steps leading up to the sinful act itself. Repeat this process with two or three other failures and see if you can identify a pattern.

- Now develop an early warning system based on the things you have identified. Share this list with the trusted friend or pastor to whom you have made yourself accountable.

Thought for the Day:

"I resolve to meet evil courageously, but when even a small temptation cometh, I am in sore straits. That which seemeth trifling sometimes giveth rise to a grievous temptation; and when I think myself to be secure, and least expect it, I am overcome by a light breath."[8]

— Thomas a Kempis

Scripture for the Day:

"So, if you think you are standing firm, be careful that you don't fall! No temptation has seized you except what is common to man. And God is faithful; he will not let you be tempted beyond what you can bear. But when you are tempted, he will also provide a way out so that you can stand up under it."

— 1 Corinthians 10:12,13

A MAN AND TEMPTATION

CHAPTER 50

OVERCOMING TEMPTATION

Temptation is a fact of life; it's inescapable. We can minimize it by practicing spiritual disciplines and avoiding obviously tempting situations, but we cannot escape it. We can, however, overcome it if we will put into practice some scriptural principles which have proved effective for generations of believers.

Principle # 1: Recognize your limitations. The Apostle Paul warns, "If you think you are standing firm, be careful that you don't fall!"[1] Many of us fall prey to sin simply because we allow ourselves to be placed in situations we cannot handle. In short, we are overconfident. To defeat temptation we must operate from a position of strength, not weakness.

Nothing illustrates this truth more clearly than the testimony of a man who overcame a lifelong battle with pornography. According to Randy Alcorn, who is pastor of small-group ministries at Good Shepherd Community Church, Gresham, Oregon, the man travels extensively. So to defeat temptation he operates from a position of strength — whenever he checks into a hotel he asks them to remove the television from his room. Invariably they look at him like he's crazy and then they usually say something like, "But sir, if you don't want to watch it, you don't have to turn it on." Since he is a paying customer he politely insists, and he has never been refused.

"The point is," he says, "I know that in my weak and lonely moments late in the evening, I'll be tempted to watch the x-rated offerings that are only one push of a button away. In the past I've succumbed to that temptation over and over, but not anymore. Having the television removed in my stronger moments has been my way of saying, 'I'm serious about this, Lord,' and it's been the key to victory in my battle against impurity."[2]

150

OVERCOMING TEMPTATION

Principle # 2: Develop an early warning system. We must become sensitive to the Holy Spirit and willing to heed His warning. To overcome temptation we must deal with it the moment it rears its ugly head. To delay is to succumb. And if we ever allow it to take root, we have lost that battle. Not the war necessarily, but definitely the battle.

Principle # 3: Hide the Word of God in your heart. It is the revelation of truth that will enable you to discern between good and evil, thus avoiding the traps of the enemy. The Word affirms your authority in Christ and declares your ability to overcome temptation.

On the cross our sinful nature, the "old self" as it were, was crucified with Christ. What we experience when temptation comes is simply the death throes of the old man. In truth, his power has been broken. He has been defeated, although not yet fully destroyed. No longer does he sit enthroned on the seat of power in our lives. Now he is on the outside begging to be restored to his former place of power. In reality, the only power he has is what we give him.

Principle # 4: Confess your temptations to someone you can trust. Over the years it has been my experience that temptation, which flourishes in secret, somehow loses much of its mesmerizing power when it is confessed and exposed to the light of Christian love. That which seems so alluring in the secrecy of your imagination is revealed for what it really is in the transparency of your confession.

Principle # 5: Flee. Some temptations, sexual temptations for example, can only be defeated by running for your life. No man is virtuous enough to resist the sexual advances of an attractive woman indefinitely. Initially, yes. Indefinitely, no!

The Old Testament story of Joseph is a case in point:

"...Now Joseph was well–built and handsome, and after a while his master's wife took notice of Joseph and said, 'Come to bed with me!'

A MAN AND TEMPTATION

"But he refused. '...My master has withheld nothing from me except you, because you are his wife. How then could I do such a wicked thing and sin against God?' And though she spoke to Joseph day after day, he refused to go to bed with her or even be with her.

"One day he went into the house to attend to his duties, and none of the household servants was inside. She caught him by his cloak and said, 'Come to bed with me!' But he left his cloak in her hand and ran out of the house."[3]

This I believe, is what Paul had in mind when he wrote, "But you, man of God, flee from all this, and pursue righteousness, godliness, faith, love, endurance and gentleness."[4]

To be sure, no one bats a thousand against temptation, and when we fail "...we have one who speaks to the Father in our defense — Jesus Christ, the Righteous One. He is the atoning sacrifice for our sins...."[5] Still, we can improve our average considerably and enhance our spiritual walk by making these five principles a part of our spiritual disciplines.

ACTION STEPS:

- Memorize these five steps:

    1) Recognize your limitations.

    2) Develop an early warning system.

    3) Hide the Word of God in your heart.

    4) Confess your temptations to someone you can trust.

    5) Flee.

- Now ask God to help you put these principles into practice day by day.

OVERCOMING TEMPTATION

Thought for the Day:

"Temptation is not something we may escape, it is essential to the full-orbed life of a man. Beware lest you think you are tempted as no one else is tempted; what you go through is the common inheritance of the race, not something no one ever went through before. God does not save us from temptations; He succours us in the midst of them."[6]

— Oswald Chambers

Scripture for the Day:

"So I say, live by the Spirit, and you will not gratify the desires of the sinful nature. For the sinful nature desires what is contrary to the Spirit, and the Spirit what is contrary to the sinful nature. They are in conflict with each other....Those who belong to Christ Jesus have crucified the sinful nature with its passions and desires. Since we live by the Spirit, let us keep in step with the Spirit."

— Galatians 5:16,17,24,25

A MAN AND HIS GOD

"If we knew how to listen to God, we would hear him speaking to us. For God does speak. He speaks in his Gospels. He also speaks through life — that new gospel to which we ourselves add a page each day. But we are rarely open to God's message, because our faith is too weak and our life too earthbound. To help us listen, at the beginning of our new intimacy with Christ, let us imagine what he would say if he himself interpreted his Gospels for the men of our day."[1]

— Michel Quoist

CHAPTER 51

CREATED IN OUR IMAGE

"**I**n the beginning," writes Spencer Marsh in *God, Man, and Archie Bunker*, "Archie created God in his own image, in his own image created he him."[2] Which is a backhanded way of suggesting that all of us have recreated God until He is more what we think He ought to be, until He is more what we are, than what He really is.

Catherine Marshall enlarges on this theme when she suggests that there is nothing so maligned in all the universe as the character of God. She says that she often hears sincere believers attribute characteristics to God that they wouldn't attribute to the meanest man in town.

I have to hang my head in shamefaced acknowledgement. I'm guilty! I've done that. I grew up thinking that God was a cross between a medieval torturer and a hanging judge. It was a kind of composite sketch I had fashioned from a half a hundred sermons, plus a lot of other misinformation I had picked up listening to misguided Christians who were forever passing off their personal prejudice as the latest word on God.

Yet, intuitively I knew better. Some saner part of me trusted God implicitly and prompted me to come to Him in my sinfulness and need. In His presence I felt loved and accepted. I was welcomed like a favored child and left secure in the knowledge that God cared and understood. No stern father or hanging judge could have made me feel that way.

In the play *The Rain Maker*, Lizzie, the daughter, speaks to a friend about her father. "Some nights I am in the kitchen washing dishes and Pop is playing poker with the boys. Well, I watch him real close, and at first I'll just see an ordinary, middle–aged man, not very interesting to look at. And then, minute by minute, I'll see little things I never saw before —good things and bad things, queer little habits I never noticed he had, ways of talking I'd never paid any mind to. Suddenly I know who he is, and I love him so much I could cry and I thank God I took time to see him real."[3]

CREATED IN OUR IMAGE

If we want to see God "real," if we really want to know Him, we will have to spend time with Him. Time apart from the clutter of our hectic lives, time alone in His presence. And then, like Lizzie, we will know Who He is, and we will love Him so much we could cry.

ACTION STEPS:

■ Write a paragraph describing your understanding of the nature and character of God.

■ Compare your paragraph with what the Bible says about God. (See Psalm 103:1–17, Jeremiah 29:11, and Hebrews 2:14–18.)

Thought for the Day:

"I'm convinced that God is not shocked by our sins. I can't think of a single sin that any of us has committed or is now practicing, that Jesus Christ did not deal with realistically in his life and sacrificially on the cross."[4]

— Bruce Larson

Scripture for the Day:

"For we do not have a high priest who is unable to sympathize with our weaknesses, but we have one who has been tempted in every way, just as we are — yet was without sin. Let us then approach the throne of grace with confidence, so that we may receive mercy and find grace to help us in our time of need."

— Hebrews 4:15,16

CHAPTER 52

A GOD CALLED FATHER

most of our misconceptions about God grow out of our personal experience and the collective experiences of others. By their very nature these experiences are subjective; therefore, they cannot be considered the final word about God. To see God as He really is, we need an objective revelation, one not tainted by human experience.

In the Library of Congress there is a copy of the U.S. Constitution which, when viewed from a certain angle, seems to bear a portrait of George Washington, the father of our country. So it is with the Scriptures. When we approach them through faith, they aren't just a collection of ancient writings, but a revelation of God Himself, a portrait of our heavenly Father.

Jesus used parables to give us a glimpse of God. For instance, He used the parable of the lost sheep to portray God as a good shepherd so concerned about the one lost sheep that He leaves the ninety–nine in the sheepfold and searches until He finds it.[1] How different from the vindictive God many of us grew up with. But how in keeping with the portrait the Word presents: "...As I live, saith the Lord God, I have no pleasure in the death of the wicked...."[2]

Not only is the God of the Scriptures compassionate and forgiving, but He is faithful as well. Paul declares, "[Even] if we are faithless, he will remain faithful, for he cannot disown himself."[3] And He is unchanging, immutable, the same yesterday, today, and forever.[4] The psalmist writes of the Lord, "In the beginning you laid the foundations of the earth, and the heavens are the work of your hands. They will perish, but you remain; they will all wear out like a garment. Like clothing you will change them and they will be discarded. But you remain the same, and your years will never end."[5]

I wish I could put into words what God is like, but I can't. In truth, I feel like the artist, William Morris, who was commissioned to paint June Burdow. He spent several hours before the canvas and finally showed it to her. It was blank except for the words, "I cannot paint you, but I love you."

God is greater than any revelation of Himself, beyond anything we can conceive. But, based on the Scriptures, I can assure you that He is too wise ever to make a mistake and too loving ever to cause one of His children to suffer a needless pain. Those who see God as He really is can confidently put their trust in Him.

ACTION STEPS:

- Read Luke 15:11–31.
- Develop a character sketch for the father in this parable by identifying his character traits (i.e., generous, merciful, forgiving, etc.)
- Now deliberately think of God as a Father with these same attributes.

Thought for the Day:

"The trouble with much of our faith is that it does not begin with God as our father, and any faith without a father is going to be hard pressed to sustain us in these difficult times."[6]

— Richard Exley

Scripture for the Day:

"For you did not receive a spirit that makes you a slave again to fear, but you received the Spirit of sonship. And by him we cry, 'Abba, Father.' The Spirit himself testifies with our spirit that we are God's children."

— Romans 8:15,16

CHAPTER 53

SEEING GOD AS HE REALLY IS

Nothing is more fundamental, more critical to our faith, than a scripturally accurate understanding of God. How we perceive Him affects everything we do — how we relate to Him in worship and service, how we relate to others, and even how we view ourselves. If we see God in any way other than how He really is, then we may spend our entire lives in an elaborate masquerade.

The Old Testament story of Abraham and Sarah is a case in point. God visited Abraham one day and told him that his wife Sarah was going to bear him a son about the same time the following year. "...Now Sarah was listening....[and] laughed to herself as she thought, 'After I am worn out and my master is old, will I now have this pleasure?'"[1]

Her laughter didn't last long. It caught in her throat when God overheard it and demanded an explanation. The Bible says, "Sarah was afraid, so she lied and said, 'I did not laugh.'...."[2]

What happened? Why was Sarah afraid? The God she knew was humorless. He was hard, and straight, and intolerant, like a stern grandfather or a hanging judge. And like many of us, she thought there was only one way to relate to Him, so she hastily donned her religious face.

This is something we seem to learn early in life. No one really says anything about it, but we get the message nonetheless. It's a subtle indoctrination wherein we are taught to say right things rather than real things, to present our religious self rather than our real self to God. As a consequence, what God intended to be an intimate relationship becomes a cheap masquerade.

SEEING GOD AS HE REALLY IS

Think for a moment and be honest. Are you natural, are you really yourself when you approach God, or do you find yourself reverting to your religious conditioning? Are your prayers conversational or pious? Formal or friendly?

John Killinger says, "The self we send out to meet God is almost always a false self."[3] Why? Because the god we worship is a false god, one created from myths and misunderstandings. Only when we see God as He really is, as He revealed Himself in Jesus Christ, can we be real with Him.

ACTION STEPS:

■ Listen to yourself the next time you pray. Are your prayers real, or are they filled with spiritual cliches?

■ Try writing your prayers in the form of a letter to God. This will encourage you to eliminate the cliches and to be very specific.

■ Write at least one prayer in which you are totally honest with God. Reveal your deepest feelings to Him.

Thought for the Day:

"What good is there to be gained by being dishonest with God? How do we ever expect to be transformed into His image if we continually cover those things we don't want God to know about?"[4]

— Bob Benson and Michael W. Benson

Scripture for the Day:

"'Woe to me!' I cried. 'I am ruined! For I am a man of unclean lips, and I live among a people of unclean lips, and my eyes have seen the King, the Lord Almighty.'

"Then one of the seraphs flew to me with a live coal in his hand, which he had taken with tongs from the altar. With it he touched my mouth and said, 'See, this has touched your lips; your guilt is taken away and your sin atoned for.'"

— Isaiah 6:5–7

CHAPTER 54

GOD'S
UNCONDITIONAL LOVE

The person who believes that God loves him, as he is, with all of his "hang–ups," believes the unbelievable. Such love is beyond us, it's too good to be true. Yet that is the heart and soul of Christianity: "...Christ died for the ungodly. Very rarely will anyone die for a righteous man, though for a good man someone might possibly dare to die. But God demonstrates his own love for us in this: *While we were still sinners, Christ died for us.*"[1]

What this literally means is that you and I are the objects of God's love but not the cause of it. God loves us, not because we are loveable, but because He is loving. His love is based on Who He is, not what we are.

"I am sure," writes A. W. Tozer of God in *The Knowledge of the Holy*, "that there is in me nothing that could attract the love of One as holy and as just as You are. Yet You have declared Your unchanging love for me in Christ Jesus. If nothing in me can win Your love, nothing in the universe can prevent You from loving me. Your love is uncaused and undeserved. You are Yourself the reason for the love wherewith I am loved."[2]

My first real understanding of God's unconditional love was born the day a wise counselor directed me to remember the most sinful thing I had ever done. Once I had that dark deed firmly fixed in my mind, he told me to think of the most loving thing, the most Christlike thing I had ever done. That was more difficult. It had been easy to remember my sinful failures, they were never far from my mind. Good deeds were another matter altogether. Still, I was finally able to think of something and I nodded.

"When," he asked me, "did God love you best? In the moment of your Christlikeness or in the moment of your sinful failure?"

GOD'S UNCONDITIONAL LOVE

In that moment I experienced a revelation of God's unconditional love. I knew, really knew, for the very first time, that God loved me best always. There was nothing I could do to make God love me more, nor was there anything I might do that could make God love me less. His love for me was infinite, eternal, and unconditional.

And with that knowledge there came a security, a confidence, that has enabled me to risk loving and living in ways I never dared before. Truly His "...perfect love drives out fear...."[3]

ACTION STEPS:

■ Recall a time when you truly felt loved by God. Meditate on that experience, live it all over again.

■ Memorize some Scriptures which talk about God's love and meditate on them. (See Psalm 86:5; 100:5; 103:17; Jeremiah 31:3; Romans 5:8.)

Thought for the Day:

"Someone has imagined God first fashioning man, and one of the host of heaven, watching, exclaiming in alarm, but you are giving this creature freedom! He will never be wise enough or strong enough to handle it. He will think himself a god. He will boast in his own self-sufficiency. How can you gamble that he will ever return to you? And God replies, I have left him unfinished within. I have left in him deep needs that only I can satisfy, that out of his desire, his homesickness of soul, he will remember to turn to me."[4]

— Frederick B. Speakman

Scripture for the Day:

"...I pray that you, being rooted and established in love, may have power, together with all the saints, to grasp how wide and long and high and deep is the love of Christ, and to know this love that surpasses knowledge — that you may be filled to the measure of all the fullness of God."

— Ephesians 3:17–19

CHAPTER 55

GIVE HIM YOUR HEART

S everal years ago I read an amazing testimony about a man named Bennie Abernathy. While in the hospital suffering from incurable cancer, he encountered God in a way which totally changed his life. No, his cancer was not miraculously cured, but something even better happened.

All his life Bennie had felt ambiguous about God. He had heard that a person must "commit his life to Christ" or "be born again" — but he didn't know how. Lying in the hospital day after day, he grew depressed. He was dying and he wanted to tie his life into God, but he didn't know what to do. In desperation he decided to pray. "God," he began haltingly, "how can I know You?"

Bennie always got choked up when he got to this part. "I saw Jesus," he would say, "here in this room, as real as you are. He was standing over there (nodding toward the corner), and there were people coming to Him. As they got to where He was, each one would reach inside his own robe and lift out his heart...and hand it to Jesus. First there were grown men, all kinds, and then there were children....And I gave Him my heart too. He took it, put His other hand on my shoulder and smiled as He said, 'peace.' And then He was gone."[1]

The last weeks of Bennie's life were filled with great suffering, but he never lost the peace that Jesus had imparted. In that mystical encounter he was able to exchange his heart, sinful though it was, for the peace of God. And freed from his sins, he was able to face death without fear.

GIVE HIM YOUR HEART

ACTION STEPS:

- If you have never given your heart to Christ, why not do it right now. Simply repeat this prayer with sincerity: "Lord Jesus, I believe that You are the Son of God. I believe that You became a man and died on the cross for my sins. I believe that God raised You from the dead and made You the Savior of the world. Now I confess my sins and ask You to forgive me, and to cleanse me of all unrighteousness. I give You my heart and I receive You as my Lord and Savior. In Jesus' name, I pray. Amen."

- Now share your experience with a trusted friend or family member.

Thought for the Day:

"There are many religions which know no divine welcome to the sinner until he has ceased to be one. They would first make him righteous, and then bid him welcome to God. But God in Christ first welcomes him, and so makes him penitent and redeems him. The one demands human righteousness as the price of divine atonement; the other makes atonement in order to evoke righteousness."[2]

— J. S. Whale

Scripture for the Day:

"...if you confess with your mouth, 'Jesus is Lord,' and believe in your heart that God raised him from the dead, you will be saved. For it is with your heart that you believe and are justified, and it is with your mouth that you confess and are saved....for, 'Everyone who calls on the name of the Lord will be saved.'"

— Romans 10:9,10,13

CHAPTER 56

SPIRITUAL GROWTH

It has been my experience that men relate to God on four basic levels. First, there is the "give me" stage. Virtually everyone starts here. Like Jacob we say, "...'If God will be with me and will watch over me on this journey I am taking and will give me food to eat and clothes to wear so that I return safely to my father's house, then the Lord will be my God."[1] When a man is in this initial stage, he is consumed with getting and loves God, as Bernard of Clairvaux observed, "...for self's sake."[2]

By the time he attains the second level in his spiritual development, the "give me" syndrome has been replaced by the "use me" syndrome. His preoccupation with getting has now evolved into an obsession to be used by God. Now he regularly prays for empowerment, and he dreams of doing great things for the Lord. He has great zeal, unfortunately, he often has little wisdom and even less love. As a consequence, he lives a life of spiritual loneliness in spite of his almost frantic involvement.

As he continues to mature in the faith, he develops a growing desire to be like Christ. During this third stage, which has been called the "make me" phase, his desire to be used by God is balanced by a yearning "...to be conformed to the likeness of his [God's] Son...."[3] Like the penitent prodigal, he now prays, " '...make me....' "[4] rather than, "give me," or even "use me."

The fourth and final phase in his relationship with God is characterized by intense love and focuses on spiritual intimacy. With the psalmist he pleads, "Search me, O God, and know my heart...."[5] Like Paul he yearns "...to know Christ and the power of his resurrection and the fellowship of...his sufferings...."[6] Now nothing is as important to him as knowing God and being known by Him.

In truth, the mature believer incorporates all four dimensions in his relationship with the Father. He trusts God to meet his daily needs without majoring in the kind of demanding prayers that often characterized their initial relationship. To him, being and becoming are now more important than mere doing. Not because he is any less zealous, but because he now understands that true ministry flows out of who he is in Christ. And more than anything he wants to know God and be known by Him.

Like the late A. W. Tozer, he prays, "Heavenly Father: Let me see your glory....whatever the cost to me in loss of friends or goods or length of days let me know you as you are, that I may adore you as I should. Through Jesus Christ our Lord. Amen."[7]

ACTION STEPS:

- Recall when you received Jesus Christ as your personal Savior.
- Take a spiritual inventory and discover where you are in your personal spiritual journey.
- Identify some specific ways you can enhance your spiritual growth.

Thought for the Day:

"For God Himself works in our souls, in their deepest depths, taking increasing control as we are progressively willing to be prepared for His wonder."[8]

— Thomas R. Kelly

Scripture for the Day:

"Then Moses said, 'Now show me your glory.'

"And the Lord said, 'I will cause all my goodness to pass in front of you, and I will proclaim my name, the Lord, in your presence....But,' he said, 'you cannot see my face, for no one may see me and live.'

"Then the Lord said, 'There is a place near me where you may stand on a rock. When my glory passes by, I will put you in a cleft in the rock and cover you with my hand until I have passed by. Then I will remove my hand and you will see my back; but my face must not be seen.'"

— Exodus 33:18–23

A MAN AND HIS PRAYER LIFE

"My hour in Carmelite chapel is more important than I can fully know myself. It is not an hour of deep prayer, nor a time in which I experience a special closeness to God; it is not a period of serious attentiveness to the divine mysteries. I wish it were! On the contrary, it is full of distractions, inner restlessness, sleepiness, confusion, and boredom. It seldom, if ever, pleases my senses. But the simple fact of being for one hour in the presence of the Lord and of showing him all that I think, feel, sense, and experience, without trying to hide anything, must please him. Somehow, somewhere, I know that he loves me, even though I do not feel that love as I can feel a human embrace, even though I do not hear a voice as I hear human words of consolation....God is greater than my senses, greater than my thoughts, greater than my heart. I do believe that he touches me in places that are unknown even to myself."[1]

— Henri J. Nouwen

CHAPTER 57

EVERYDAY PRAYERS

Best–selling author, Betty Malz, says, "For many years I directed my prayers toward the large and important things....I thought God must have a good sense of humor to put up with all the trifling 'piffleberries' people threw at Him.

Her paternal grandmother was the first to successfully challenge Betty's thinking. "Betty," she would say, "you have not because you ask not."

"But," Betty would protest, "God gave us intelligence to handle the small matters."

Her grandmother simply shook her head. "We need Him for all things. Why once I couldn't find my nutmeg and I asked the Lord to find it for me. In exactly six minutes Mrs. Green was at my door. She said, 'Mrs. Perkins, I borrowed this nutmeg weeks ago and forgot to return it. Why, just this minute I remembered to bring it back.' "[2]

That kind of prayer works for men too. Some time ago we were facing a financial crisis in our radio ministry. Finally, after weeks of worry, I decided to pray about it. I surrendered the ministry to God anew and told Him that if He no longer wanted us to do it that I would willingly discontinue it. "If You want us to continue," I prayed, "then You will have to supernaturally supply the needed funds."

Later that morning a longtime supporter of the "Straight From the Heart" broadcast came into my office and handed me a check for $9,300. When I glanced at it I realized that it was dated almost a week earlier. When I commented on it he told me that he had been carrying it in his wallet for several days, but that he just hadn't had time to get by my office. I was immediately reminded of God's promise: "Before they call I will answer; while they are still speaking I will hear."[3]

Of course, I'm not talking about turning God into some kind of cosmic Santa Claus. But if we pray God–centered prayers, there is always a place for our personal needs. He Who taught us to pray, "...your kingdom come...," also taught us to pray, "...give us today our daily bread...."[4]

In prayer, as in all of life, there must be a balance between daily bread and coming kingdoms. He who spends time in prayer getting to know God, thinking God's thoughts after Him, will never be guilty of praying petty, selfish prayers. Yet, on the other hand he will never be embarrassed to share with the Father the concerns of his heart, regardless of how insignificant they might seem.

In true prayer, we receive both a revelation of God's character and a manifestation of His goodness:

> "Thou art coming to a king
> Large petitions with thee bring,
> For His wealth and power are such
> That thou canst never ask too much."[5]

Or too little, I might add.

ACTION STEPS:

- Take a few minutes right now and recall some specific answers to prayer.
- If you or those you love have specific needs at this time, great or small, make a list of them and simply ask God to divinely intervene.

Thought for the Day:

"...prayer is neither chiefly begging for things, nor is it merely self-communion; it is that loftiest experience within the reach of any soul, communion with God."[6]

— Harry Emerson Fosdick

Scripture for the Day:

"Now to him who is able to do immeasurably more than all we ask or imagine, according to his power that is at work within us, to him be glory in the church and in Christ Jesus throughout all generations, for ever and ever! Amen."

— Ephesians 3:20,21

CHAPTER 58

PRAYERS GOD CANNOT ANSWER

rederick Speakman tells the story of a little girl who rushed home from her geography examination to glance hurriedly at a map, then dropped to her knees with the earnest petition, "Dear God, quick, make Boston the capital of Vermont!" Now God may have enjoyed that request. But, at last report He has not granted it. It was cute, but it wasn't Christian because it was not the kind of prayer our kind of God could grant!

John says, "...if we ask anything according to his will, he hears us."[1]

That's the key, isn't it? — asking according to God's will. No matter how much faith we exercise, God will not grant petitions that violate His holy character. Nor will He give us the desires of our heart if doing so does not contribute to our eternal good.

As a boy I loved Mom's homemade peach cobbler. That is, until the time I ate too much and got sick. I remember the fateful incident well. After finishing one heaping bowlful I asked for a second helping, promptly polished it off, and then asked for a third. At this point Mother tried to reason with me. Too much of a good thing, she pointed out, might make me sick.

"Not a chance," I said.

"It's very rich," she explained patiently, "especially with all that cream."

"Please," I begged, "just one more helping."

At last Mother capitulated and I dug into my third bowl of peach cobbler and thick country cream. Unfortunately, she proved to be a prophet, and sometime in the night I awoke in deep distress and barely made it into the bathroom before vomiting.

PRAYERS GOD CANNOT ANSWER

That painfully humorous incident, I believe, illustrates the kind of prayers our heavenly Father cannot grant. He loves us too much to grant our self–destructive petitions. Not infrequently that frustrates me, at least initially, but in the end I appreciate His wisdom and the protection it provides.

ACTION STEPS:

■ Ask yourself these questions: Are my prayers compatible with the character of God? Are they the kind of petitions God can grant without violating His nature?

■ Think of a time when God changed your thoughts and desires as you prayed. Has time given you a chance to see how things worked out for the best? List these ways.

■ Develop the habit of inviting God to purify your prayers, to express His wisdom and His will through them.

Thought for the Day:

"Lord, I know not what I ought to ask of Thee; Thou only knowest what I need; Thou lovest me better than I know how to love myself....Pray Thyself in me. Amen."[2]

— Francois Fenelon

Scripture for the Day:

"During the days of Jesus' life on earth, he offered up prayers and petitions with loud cries and tears to the one who could save him from death, and he was heard because of his reverent submission."

— Hebrews 5:7

CHAPTER 59

PRAYING THROUGH

What Jacob experienced the night that he wrestled with God, in the dark, on the muddy bank of the Jabbok, was true prayer — life–changing prayer! "Then the man said, 'Your name will no longer be Jacob, but Israel, because you have struggled with God and with men and have overcome.' "[1]

We used to have prayer meetings like that. "Praying through" we called it, which meant that we weren't leaving the place of prayer until God had touched us, cleansed us, made us new! Like Jacob, we determined, "...'I will not let you go unless you bless me.' "[2]

There's an element of truth in the popular teaching on prayer which says to ask, believe, and receive, to "confess and possess." But if we ever forget the widow's importunity (Luke 18:1–8), or the empty–handed host's midnight persistence (Luke 11:5–8), or Jacob's stubborn determination (Genesis 32:22–30), we will have lost an irreplaceable part of our birthright. "...The effectual fervent prayer of a righteous man [still] availeth much."[3]

This kind of serious, intense prayer reminds me of something Emilie Griffin wrote in *Clinging — The Experience of Prayer:* "Prayer is," she writes, "after all, a very dangerous business. For all the benefits it offers of growing closer to God, it carries with it one great element of risk: the possibility of change. *In prayer we open ourselves to the chance that God will do something with us that we had not intended....*

"Don't we know for a fact that people who begin by 'just praying' — with no particular aim in mind — wind up trudging off to missionary lands, entering monasteries, taking part in demonstrations, dedicating themselves to the poor and the sick?...Isn't this what holds us back — the knowledge of God's omnipotence, his unguessability, his power, his right to ask All of us, a perfect gift of self, a perfect act of full surrender?"[4]

Yet finally, isn't this what also brings *us* to see "...God face to face...,"[5] the knowledge of His omnipotence, His unguessability, His power, His right to ask ALL of us, His ability to ultimately deliver us from our selfish selves, to make us new in every way?

PRAYING THROUGH

ACTION STEPS:

■ Remember, if you can, a prayer experience where you "prayed through." Write a few sentences describing your experience.

■ Ask God to teach you to pray with that kind of determined intensity.

■ List the major issues you are facing in your life at this time. Now set aside some specific time so you can "pray through" on these important issues.

Thought for the Day:

"...The image of struggle, the emphasis on earnest perseverance, certainly expresses faith, in that it makes the believer an intimate of God. But it is a short step from prayer as wrestling with God to prayer as a means of pressure or act of magic....Our intercession must always oscillate somewhat between these two emphases. Faith is simultaneously long perseverance and unwavering confidence. If prayer is too much involved with insisting, it no longer addresses itself to the true God; if it is too quickly and too easily confident, it no longer expresses us truly."[6]

— Pierre–Yves Emery

Scripture for the Day:

"Going a little farther, he fell to the ground and prayed that if possible the hour might pass from him. 'Abba, Father,' he said, 'everything is possible for you. Take this cup from me. Yet not what I will, but what you will."

— Mark 14:35,36

CHAPTER 60

THE SILENCE OF GOD

or many of us, silence is uncomfortable, even frightening. Therefore, we succumb to the temptation to fill our lives, and our relationships, with a noisy busyness. Conversation becomes our primary way of communicating, and we end up exchanging information without really relating to one another. After a while this may seem normal, but it is not fulfilling.

The same thing happens in our relationship with God. Worship and prayer, which were designed to still us before the Lord, are turned into things we "do" rather than opportunities to "be still and know." As a consequence, silence is lost; then, by virtue of its absence, it becomes foreign. And without that holy stillness our spiritual life is diminished, for silence has always been characteristic of a truly intimate relationship with the Lord.

In order to recover the renewing power of holy silence, we must first come to terms with it. Silence is not an enemy to be avoided, but a friend to be embraced. It is the language of the soul, the language of intimacy. Even as the heart speaks through silence, so God also speaks to the heart through silence. In silence God teaches us the deep mysteries of the Spirit, the things that can never be communicated with mere words.

Initially our relationship with God, like the rest of our life, is filled with noisy busyness, but as we become more intimate the silence deepens, and in the silence God speaks to us as a friend with a friend.[1] And slowly, ever so slowly, over months and sometimes years, we come to understand the wisdom of His silence. In truth, the most profound and holy things God communicates to men are often communicated in silence as "Deep calls to deep...."[2]

ACTION STEPS:

- Take your lunch hour and spend it sitting in silent contemplation in an empty chapel or sanctuary.
- Since silence is so foreign to most of us, you may have to repeat that discipline for several days in a row before it becomes truly meaningful.

Thought for the Day:

"A common problem, related to why we may seek to escape silence, is the discovery that it evokes nameless misgivings, guilt feelings, strange, disquieting anxiety. Anything is better than this mess, and so we flick on the radio or pick up the phone and talk to a friend. If we can pass through these initial fears and remain silent, we may experience a gradual waning of inner chaos. Silence becomes like a creative space in which we regain perspective on the whole."[3]

— Susan Annette Muto

"My father himself never talked to me, except when we studied together. He taught me with silence....When his people would ask him why he was so silent with his son, he would say to them that he did not like to talk, words are cruel, words play tricks, they distort what is in the heart, they conceal the heart, the heart speaks through silence."[4]

— Chaim Potok

Scripture for the Day:

"The Lord said, 'Go out and stand on the mountain in the presence of the Lord, for the Lord is about to pass by.'

"Then a great and powerful wind tore the mountains apart and shattered the rocks before the Lord, but the Lord was not in the wind. After the wind there was an earthquake, but the Lord was not in the earthquake. After the earthquake came a fire, but the Lord was not in the fire. And after the fire came a gentle whisper. When Elijah heard it, he pulled his cloak over his face and went out and stood at the mouth of the cave...."

— 1 Kings 19:11–13

CHAPTER 61

KNOWING GOD THROUGH PRAYER

There are several ways that a person may grow in his knowledge of the Lord. The Scriptures provide a written revelation of God, fellowship is a living revelation, and then there's prayer. Not just any kind of prayer, but lingering prayer, listening prayer. For as Abraham Joshua Heschel says, "Mindfulness of God arises slowly, a thought at a time."[1]

As we wait before God in holy quietness, something happens. We experience a growing awareness, a sense that we are not alone though no other person is in the room with us. There is an awakening deep within, a stirring, what the psalmist refers to as "Deep calling unto deep...."[2] An old mystic described it as God putting His face against the windowpane of our lives, or as Jacob said, " '...I saw God face to face....' "[3] In prayer God can become that real to us.

How small our past prayers now seem. We have been praying about petty concerns, hangnails, and other little hurts, when we might have been seeking a revelation of His holiness. Don't misunderstand me. I'm not saying we shouldn't pray for daily bread. I'm simply suggesting that we rob ourselves if that's all we pray about.

In *A Diary of Private Prayer*, John Baillie prayed, "...grant me, I pray you, a clearer vision of your truth, a greater faith in your power, and a more confident assurance of your love."[4] And if we desire to know God, intimately, personally, that is the kind of prayer we too must pray:

"Speak to Him, thou, for He hears,
And Spirit with spirit can meet,
Closer is He than breathing,
And nearer than hands and feet."[5]

KNOWING GOD THROUGH PRAYER

ACTION STEPS:

- Spend five to ten minutes in listening prayer right now.
- Be aware of your feelings and impressions, even more than your thoughts, for God often speaks to us through our senses rather than through our intellect.
- Record your impressions. Did God direct you to a family concern that needs your attention? Did God address some issue in your inner life, some attitude that needs to be corrected? This is often how God speaks to us when we take the time to listen in prayer.

Thought for the Day:

"It is not objective proof of God's existence that we want but, whether we use religious language for it or not, the experience of God's presence. That is the miracle that we are really after. And that is also, I think, the miracle that we really get."[6]

— Frederick Buechner

Scripture for the Day:

"As the deer pants for streams of water,
so my soul pants for you, O God.
My soul thirsts for God, for the living God.
When can I go and meet with God?"

— Psalm 42:1,2

A MAN AND HIS CHRISTIAN SERVICE

"The mystery of ministry is that the Lord is to be found where we minister. That is what Jesus tells us when he says: 'Insofar as you did this to one of the least of these brothers of mine, you did it to me' (Matt. 25:40). Our care for people thus becomes the way to meet the Lord. The more we give, help, support, guide, counsel, and visit, the more we receive, not just similar gifts, but the Lord himself. To go to the poor is to go to the Lord. Living this truth in our daily life makes it possible to care for people without conditions, without hesitation, without suspicion, or without the need for immediate rewards. With this sacred knowledge, we can avoid becoming burned out."[1]

— Henri J. Nouwen

CHAPTER 62

SOMETHING TO LIVE FOR

Few things in life are more elusive than fulfillment. All of us have known highly successful people who, for all of their achievements, have not found personal satisfaction. In the most extreme cases they end up embittered old men living out their days in lonely isolation. How, I often ask myself, can someone so successful be so unhappy?

One of the most tragic examples is King Solomon. He had everything — wealth, wisdom, worldwide recognition, and an ever–deepening misery. Hear him as he laments the emptiness of life: "I have seen all the things that are done under the sun; all of them are meaningless, a chasing after the wind."[2]

Describing his unbridled pursuit of pleasure he confesses, "I denied myself nothing my eyes desired; I refused my heart no pleasure....But that also proved to be meaningless."[3]

If he were only another rich playboy, his emptiness would be easier to understand, but he's not. He's the head of state, the King of Israel, a gifted man who literally transformed those twelve nomadic tribes into a world power. His domestic programs made Israel the envy of all her neighbors. He undertook great projects and amassed enormous wealth, yet without experiencing personal fulfillment:

"...I built houses for myself and planted vineyards. I made gardens and parks and planted all kinds of fruit trees in them. I made reservoirs to water groves of flourishing trees. I amassed silver and gold for myself, and the treasure of kings and provinces. I acquired men and women singers, and a harem as well — the delights of the heart of man. Yet when I surveyed all that my hands had done and what I had toiled to achieve, everything was meaningless, a chasing after the wind; nothing was gained under the sun."[4]

Now contrast his empty futility with the vibrancy evidenced in this letter penned by an early Christian martyr: "In a dark hole I have found cheerfulness; in a place of bitterness and death I have found rest. While others weep I have found laughter, where others fear I have found strength. Who would believe that in a state of misery I have had great pleasure; that in a lonely corner I have had glorious company, and in the hardest bonds perfect repose. All those things Jesus has granted me. He is with me, comforts me, and fills me with joy. He drives bitterness from me and fills me with strength and consolation."[5]

What's the difference? How can this man, imprisoned and facing death, be filled with such joyous optimism, while Solomon is miserable in the midst of his wealth and power? To find the answer we will have to look deeper than the outward trappings of their lives.

What we are talking about here is a man's motives, his reason for living. If a man lives only for himself he will soon grow sick of himself. But if he lives for God and others, without seeking his own happiness, he will soon discover the joy of living. Noted psychologist, William James, often said, "The only truly happy people I know are those who have found a cause to live for which is greater than themselves."

ACTION STEPS:

- Think of two or three truly happy people. Now examine their lives to see if you can discover the "secret" of their happiness.

- Examine your own life. Are you living for yourself? Do you spend a lot of emotional energy making sure others treat you right, making sure you get your "fair" share? If so, take the next few minutes to list ways in which you do this and then repent of them one by one. Now ask God to help you live for Christ and others rather than for yourself.

- Remember that personal happiness is a consequence, not a goal. Seek for it, and you will never find it. Give it to others, and it will find you.

Thought for the Day:

"It is a very small matter to you whether the man gives you your right or not: it is life or death to you whether or not you give him his."[6]

— George MacDonald

Scripture for the Day:

" 'Whoever finds his life will lose it, and whoever loses his life for my sake will find it.' "

— Matthew 10:39

CHAPTER 63

TRANSCENDING OUR LIMITATIONS

I often feel overwhelmed in face of the world's enormous need. I mean, what can one person do about world hunger, or the homeless, or unemployment, or abortion on demand, or the billions who have never heard the Gospel of Jesus Christ? Not infrequently I am tempted to conclude that if I can't fix everything, why should I try to fix anything?

Norman Cousins refutes such misguided reasoning in his book *Human Options*: "Certainly it is true that behind every human being who cries out for help there may be a million or more equally entitled to attention. But this is the poorest of all reasons for not helping the person whose cries you hear....Reach out and take hold of the one who happens to be nearest. If you are never able to help or save another, at least you will have saved one."[1]

Nor should we ever make light of what God can do with our faithful efforts, regardless of how insignificant they may seem. Take Lizzie Johnson for instance. "At thirteen Lizzie injured her back in an accident, and she was to spend the rest of her life, twenty–seven more years, flat on her back. Her only view of the world was from a mirror mounted above her head. But she still wanted to do a great thing with her life, so when she heard in those days that you could free an African slave for $40, she made a quilt and tried to sell it for $40. Nobody would buy it. So she turned to making bookmarks, and she raised $1,000 a year for each of the twenty–seven years remaining in her life. She gave every penny of that to projects in this world that go to building up rather than tearing down.

TRANSCENDING OUR LIMITATIONS

"What about the quilt? One day a bishop from India was traveling through Illinois and she gave it to him. He took that quilt with him on his speaking tour around the country, and he told the story of Lizzie Johnson. Then he asked people if they would place an offering for missions in the quilt. He raised $100,000 for missions. You talk about how God creates miracles through modest efforts!

"One day after Lizzie Johnson had died, her sister, Alice Johnson, heard that a man named Takuo Matsumoto was coming to Champaign, Illinois, to speak. He was one of the most prominent Japanese Christians after the Second World War. He had been principal of the Methodist Girls' School in Hiroshima during the bombing. In John Hersey's book about tragedy, he is mentioned prominently as one of the heroes of those days.

"Alice Johnson remembered that her sister had given money to support the education of a young boy in Japan named Takuo Matsumoto, and she wondered if this was the same person. She resolved to go to Champaign to hear him speak, but she got sick that day and had to stay home. That night someone told Mr. Matsumoto about her, and he said, 'You mean that she is Lizzie Johnson's sister? All that I am I owe to Lizzie Johnson.' That night he went to see Alice Johnson, and he went from there to the cemetery to put flowers on the grave of a woman who could not leave her bed, who was weak and helpless, but who stitched up her love in bookmarks and quilts and said, 'Thank you, God,' by loving others."[2]

If God could use Lizzie Johnson's feeble, but faithful, efforts to achieve so much, then surely He can do something with our acts of compassion as well, be they great or small.

A MAN AND HIS CHRISTIAN SERVICE

ACTION STEPS:

■ Ask God to open your eyes so that you can see the needy He has placed in your path. Ask Him to open your ears so you can hear their cries. Now make a list of the needs He has brought to your attention.

■ Ask God to show you how you can minister to these needs. Make a list of the thoughts that come to your mind. Don't eliminate any possibilities at this point. Give your imagination free rein.

■ Over the next several days consider these possibilities prayerfully and then begin investing yourself. Don't be afraid of starting small. Remember, anything is better than nothing.

Thought for the Day:

"God has a history of using the insignificant to accomplish the impossible."

— Richard Exley

TRANSCENDING OUR LIMITATIONS

Scripture for the Day:

"When Jesus looked up and saw a great crowd coming toward him, he said to Philip, 'Where shall we buy bread for these people to eat?' He asked this only to test him, for he already had in mind what he was going to do.

"Philip answered him, 'Eight months' wages would not buy enough bread for each one to have a bite!'"

Another of his disciples, Andrew, Simon Peter's brother, spoke up, 'Here is a boy with five small barley loaves and two small fish, but how far will they go among so many?'

"Jesus said, 'Have the people sit down.' There was plenty of grass in that place, and the men sat down, about five thousand of them. Jesus then took the loaves, gave thanks, and distributed to those who were seated as much as they wanted. He did the same with the fish.

"When they had all had enough to eat, he said to his disciples, 'Gather the pieces that are left over. Let nothing be wasted.' So they gathered them and filled twelve baskets with the pieces of the five barley loaves left over by those who had eaten."

— John 6:5–13

CHAPTER 64

KEEPERS OF THE FAITH

If you grew up attending Sunday school and church, I want you to take a minute and think of those people who shaped your faith. One of the first persons who comes to my mind is LuElla Headly. She taught the beginner Sunday school class when I was just a boy. Although our Sunday school class was located in the church basement, in a musty room under the stairs, she had a way of transforming it into a vibrant learning center.

Her most effective teaching tool was the peep box. She created it by lining the inside of a shoe box with full–color scenes illustrating stories from the Bible. Next, she took cut–out figures of Bible characters and pasted them to the bottom of the box so they stood upright, creating a three–dimensional effect. Finally, she covered the top of the shoe box with white tissue paper.

Each week when I placed my eye against the half–dollar–sized peep hole in the end of that shoe box I was transported into another time and place. No longer was I sitting in that musty room beneath the stairs. Now I was standing with Moses on Mount Sinai. I was with Isaiah in the temple. I was with Jesus in Gethsemane. In that moment the Scripture lesson came alive for me.

In truth, LuElla is just one of several Sunday school teachers who had a profound influence on that young boy's life. Others included Ralph Eldridge, Leonard Ford, Harvey Lee Clark, and my wife's mother, Hildegarde Wallace. And I was just one of scores of young men and women whose lives were shaped by their faithful service.

Donald MacLeod tells about a common laborer in the little village of Blantyre, Scotland. His name was David Hogg and year after year he taught a small Sunday school class of young boys with a devotion that was the wonder of all who knew him.

"Out from that class went a young man, David Livingston, to the vast continent of Africa to wear out his life, going through the jungles from village to village, witnessing to the Christian faith. Some time later another missionary came to one of these same villages where Livingston had been years before, and he told of the life and ministry of Jesus Christ. An old lady, however, interrupted him and said, 'That man has been here!'

"Think of it: ...a village church in far away Scotland; a little boy in the sanctuary; a consecrated Sunday school teacher; and you get the footprints of Christ in and out of the muddy villages of Africa."[1]

I dare say that David Hogg had no idea that his dedicated teaching would play a vital part in shaping the spiritual life of David Livingston. Or that David Livingston would be used significantly by God to evangelize the continent of Africa. Indeed, only eternity will reveal the contributions made by faithful Sunday school teachers the world over. They are the unsung heros of the Kingdom and the keepers of our faith.

As I think about those dedicated Sunday school teachers whose faithful service shaped my own faith, I am moved almost to tears. I wish there was some way I could pay them back, some way to let them know that because of their godly influence I am a writer and minister today. Perhaps there's a better way. Maybe love like theirs is not to be paid back but passed on.

ACTION STEPS:

- Make a list of the people who have had the most profound influence on your life, especially your spiritual life.
- Identify specific things they did that shaped your character and your faith. Your list should include things as seemingly insignificant as listening to you, as well as things like modeling the Christian life.
- Now make a commitment to God that you will pass their love and influence on to the next generation.

Thought for the Day:

"Eric Hoffer tells a story about a Bavarian peasant woman who cared for him after his mother died and during the years that he was blind: 'And this woman, this Martha took care of me. She was a big woman, with a small head. And this woman, this Martha, must have really loved me, because those eight years of blindness are in my mind as a happy time. I remember a lot of talk and laughter. I must have talked a great deal, because Martha used to say again and again, 'You remember you said this, you remember you said that...' She remembered everything I said, and all my life I've had the feeling that what I think and what I say are worth remembering. She gave me that....'[2]

— Elizabeth O'Connor

Scripture for the Day:

"'And if anyone gives a cup of cold water to one of these little ones because he is my disciple, I tell you the truth, he will certainly not lose his reward.'"

— Matthew 10:42

CHAPTER 65

BLUE–COLLAR CHRISTIANITY

I n our house, Christianity wasn't a moral code, church membership, or a way of behaving in public. It was a lifestyle — love with its sleeves rolled up! If there was a job to do, we did it. If there was a need, we did our best to meet it. Pleasing God and serving others was our highest goal.

Once when I was still in elementary school, we came out of church after prayer meeting on a Wednesday night and saw a transient family in a beat–up old car parked in front of the church. They looked tired, and a hungry baby whimpered from the broken–down back seat. Even as a child, I could see the hollow look in their eyes, the quiet desperation that had prematurely aged their faces, leaving them flat and empty. They were good people, just down on their luck, and too proud to ask for help. Still, it was obvious that they were hoping some of the Lord's people would have compassion on them.

Dad did. He walked right over to the driver's side of the car, stuck out his hand, and introduced himself. He invited them home for supper, although it was long past supper time, and told them they could spend the night with us.

We didn't have much ourselves, as I recall, but my folks were always more than willing to share what little we had, and soon the kitchen was full of friendly smells. Mother put together a simple meal of homemade bread, fried potatoes, and ham. I followed Dad down into the half–finished basement where we collected two quarts of home–canned peaches for dessert. As we ascended the stairs, I distinctly remember the sound of ham sizzling in the skillet. Since that night it's always sounded like love to me, a good sound, friendly and comforting.

Another time Dad remodeled a small house for a young widow and her two children. Her husband, Merl, had died suddenly of a brain tumor, leaving her with almost nothing. Following the funeral, she was forced to move into more affordable housing and the only thing she could find was a small house which was desperately in need of repair.

BLUE–COLLAR CHRISTIANITY

When Dad learned about her situation, he offered to help. Night after night, for several weeks, we two boys and Mom accompanied him as he replaced the plumbing, put in new wiring, built cupboards for the kitchen, and repainted inside and out. Finally he was finished and that young mother and her two children had a small but comfortable place to call home. More than that, they knew they were not alone, that God had not forgotten them!

I call that blue–collar Christianity, and I think that's what James had in mind when he wrote, "Religion that God our Father accepts as pure and faultless is this: to look after orphans and widows in their distress and to keep oneself from being polluted by the world."[1]

ACTION STEPS:
■ Christian service isn't just something to talk about, it's something to do! Can you think of someone who needs your help — a young boy who needs a father figure to spend time with him; an elderly widow whose house needs some minor maintenance or repairs; or someone in the hospital who needs a visit? Now make an appointment on your calendar and do it.

■ Consider organizing a Christian Service Committee at your church to address needs like these in a systematic way.

Thought for the Day:
Once St. Augustine was asked, "What does love look like?" He answered:
"It has hands to help others.
It has feet to hasten to the poor and needy.
It has eyes to see misery and want.
It has ears to hear the sighs and sorrow of men.
That is what love looks like."[2]

— St. Augustine

Scripture for the Day:
"Command them to do good, to be rich in good deeds, and to be generous and willing to share. In this way they will lay up treasure for themselves as a firm foundation for the coming age, so that they may take hold of the life that is truly life."

— 1 Timothy 6:18,19

ENDNOTES

CHAPTER 1

[1]Susan Annette Muto, *Pathways of Spiritual Living*, quoted in *Disciplines for the Inner Life* by Bob Benson and Michael W. Benson (Waco: Word Books Publisher, 1985), p. 170.

[2]Richard Foster, *The Freedom of Simplicity* (San Francisco: Harper and Row Publishers, 1981), pp. 91,92.

[3]*Ibid.*, p. 92.

[4]Jeremy Taylor, quoted in *Disciplines for the Inner Life* by Bob Benson and Michael W. Benson (Waco: Word Books Publisher, 1985), p. 22.

CHAPTER 2

[1]Richard Foster, *The Freedom of Simplicity* (San Francisco: Harper and Row Publishers, 1981), pp. 80,81.

[2]Thomas R. Kelly, *A Testament of Devotion* (San Francisco: Harper and Row Publishers, 1941), p. 109.

CHAPTER 3

[1]Richard Exley, *Rhythm of Life* (Tulsa: Honor Books, 1987).

[2]Henri J. Nouwen, *Out of Solitude*, quoted in *Disciplines for the Inner Life* by Bob Benson and Michael W. Benson (Waco: Word Books Publisher, 1985), p. 35.

CHAPTER 4

[1]M. Basil Pennington, *A Place Apart*, quoted in *Disciplines for the Inner Life* by Bob Benson and Michael W. Benson (Waco: Word Books Publisher, 1985), p. 328.

CHAPTER 5

[1]Matthew 23:11.

[2]David Shibley, *Heavenly Incentives For Earthly Living* (Old Tappan: Fleming H. Revell Company, Chosen Books, 1988), p. 24.

CHAPTER 6

[1]Max Lerner, quoted in *The Relational Revolution* by Bruce Larson (Waco: Word Books Publisher, 1976), p. 133.

[2]Luke 12:22,30,31.

[3]Richard Exley, *The Rhythm of Life* (Tulsa: Honor Books, 1987), p. 20.

CHAPTER 7

[1]Anthony Campolo, *Who Switched the Price Tags?* (Waco: Word Books Publisher, 1986), p. 111.

[2]A. W. Tozer, *The Pursuit of God* (Harrisburg: Christian Publications, Inc., 1948), p. 127.

[3]Ben Patterson, *The Grand Essentials* (Waco: Word Books Publisher, 1987), p. 23.

CHAPTER 8

[1]Ben Patterson, *The Grand Essentials* (Waco: Word Books Publisher, 1987), p. 57.

CHAPTER 9

[1]John Bisagno, *Positive Obedience* (Grand Rapids: Zondervan, 1979), quoted in "Pastor's Professional Research Service."

[2]Philippians 2:3,4.

[3]Dwain Jones, *Take This Job and Love It!*, quoted in *Pleasing God, Pleasing You,* compiled and edited by Hal Donaldson and Kenneth M. Dobson (Visalia: Onward Books, 1992), p. 164.

CHAPTER 10

[1]Harold Kushner, *When All You've Ever Wanted Isn't Enough* (New York: Summit Books, A Division of Simon and Schuster, Inc., 1986), pp. 109,110.

CHAPTER 11

[1]Richard Exley, *Blue–Collar Christianity* (Tulsa: Honor Books, 1989), p. 67.

CHAPTER 12

[1]James Humes, *Churchill: Speaker of the Century* (Briarcliff Manor, New York: Stein and Day, Scarborough House, 1980), p. 291.

[2]R. Kent Hughes, *Disciplines of a Godly Man* (Wheaton: Crossway Books, 1991), pp. 35,36.

[3]Arthur Gordon, *A Touch of Wonder* (Old Tappan: Fleming H. Revell Company, 1974), p. 20.

CHAPTER 13

[1]Dorothy T. Samuel, *Fun and Games in Marriage* (Waco: Word Books Publisher, 1973), p. 21.

[2]James Dobson, *Dr. Dobson Answers Your Questions* (Wheaton: Tyndale House Publishers, 1982), p. 329.

[3]Dorothy T. Samuel, *Fun and Games in Marriage* (Waco: Word Books Publisher, 1973), p. 23.

CHAPTER 14

[1]Richard Exley, *Perils of Power* (Tulsa: Honor Books, 1988), p. 43.

CHAPTER 15

[1]Genesis 4:1 KJV.

[2]Desmond Morris, *Intimate Behavior* (New York: Random House, 1971), p. 73.

[3]H. Norman Wright, *Understanding the Man in Your Life* (Waco: Word Books Publisher, 1987), p. 195.

CHAPTER 16

[1]Ephesians 4:26 KJV.

[2]H. Norman Wright, *Communication: Key to Your Marriage* (Ventura: Regal Books, 1974), p. 145.

CHAPTER 17

[1]Ephesians 5:23–25.

[2]Jack and Carole Mayhall, *Marriage Takes More Than Love* (Colorado Springs: Navpress, 1978), p. 167.

[3]Joyce Caloney, "Confessions of a Happy Housewife," *Reader's Digest*, April 1982.

CHAPTER 18

[1]These thoughts are based on material from *Marriage Takes More Than Love* by Jack and Carole Mayhall (Colorado Springs: Navpress, 1978), Ch. 24–28.

[2]James 1:5.

[3]Gordon MacDonald, *Rebuilding Your Broken World* (Nashville: Oliver Nelson, A Division of Thomas Nelson Publishers, 1988), p. 157.

[4]Jack and Carole Mayhall, *Marriage Takes More Than Love* (Colorado Springs: Navpress, 1978), p. 186.

CHAPTER 19

[1]R. Kent Hughes, *Disciplines of a Godly Man* (Wheaton: Crossway Books, 1991), p. 55.

CHAPTER 20

[1]James C. Dobson, *Straight Talk to Men and Their Wives* (Waco: Word Books Publisher, 1980), pp. 13,14.

CHAPTER 21

[1]Quoted in *Encyclopedia of 7,700 Illustrations: Signs of the Times* by Paul Lee Tan, (Chicago: Assurance Publishers, 1979), p. 433.

CHAPTER 22

[1]Jeremiah 1:5 NAS.

[2]Luke 1:15.

[3]R. Kent Hughes, *Disciplines of a Godly Man* (Wheaton: Crossway Books, 1991), p. 49.

CHAPTER 23

[1]Cecil G. Osborne, *The Art of Becoming a Whole Person* (Waco: Word Books Publisher, 1978), p. 99.

CHAPTER 24

[1]1 Samuel 2:12.

[2]1 Samuel 8:3.

[3]1 Samuel 3:13.

[4]Paul Lee Tan, *Encyclopedia of 7,700 Illustrations: Signs of the Times* (Chicago: Assurance Publishers, 1979), p. 431.

CHAPTER 25

[1]Deuteronomy 6:6,7.

[2]Matthew 22:37–40.

[3]Ecclesiastes 12:13.

[4]Proverbs 3:5,6.

[5]*New American Standard Bible Reference Edition* (Chicago: Moody Press), p. 526.

[6]R. Kent Hughes, *Disciplines of a Godly Man* (Wheaton: Crossway Books, 1991), p. 56.

CHAPTER 26

[1]Cecil G. Osborne, *The Art of Becoming a Whole Person* (Waco: Word Books Publisher, 1978), p. 117.

CHAPTER 27

[1]Arthur Gordon, *A Touch of Wonder* (Old Tappan: Fleming H. Revell Company, 1974), pp. 52,53.

CHAPTER 28

[1]James Houston, *The Transforming Friendship* (Batavia: Lion Publishing Corporation, 1989), pp. 13,14.

[2]Paul D. Robbins, "Must Men Be Friendless?" *Leadership*, Fall 1984, p. 28.

CHAPTER 29

[1]C. D. Prentice, quoted in *Tapestries of Life* edited by Phyllis Hobe (New York: A. J. Holman Company, 1974), p. 36.

[2]Paraphrased from *Building Relationships That Last: Life's Bottom Line* by Richard Exley (Tulsa: Honor Books, 1990), p. 233.

CHAPTER 30

[1]1 Samuel 18:1,3,4.

[2]1 Samuel 18:1.

[3]1 Samuel 18:3.

[4]C. S. Lewis, quoted in "Must Men Be Friendless?" by Paul D. Robbins, *Leadership*, Fall 1984, p. 28.

[5]1 Samuel 23:17.

[6]Terry C. Muck, "From the Editor," *Leadership*, Fall 1984, p. 3.

CHAPTER 31

[1]Charles Ludwig, *He Freed Britain's Slaves* (Scottdale: Herald Press, 1977), p. 146.

[2]*Ibid.*, dustjacket.

[3]Tilden H. Edwards, "Living Simply Through the Day," quoted in *Disciplines for the Inner Life* by Bob Benson and Michael W. Benson (Waco: Word Book Publisher, 1985), p. 104.

CHAPTER 32

[1]Keith Miller and Bruce Larson, *Living the Adventure* (Waco: Word Books Publisher, 1975), p. 116.

[2]Based on information contained in *Encyclopedia of 7,700 Illustrations: Signs of the Times* by Paul Lee Tan (Chicago: Assurance Publishers, 1979), p. 824.

[3]1 Timothy 6:17.

[4]1 Timothy 6:9,10.

[5]Matthew 6:25,32,33.

[6]1 Timothy 6:18,19.

[7]Luke 6:38.

[8]Keith Miller and Bruce Larson, *Living the Adventure* (Waco: Word Books Publisher, 1975), pp. 117,118.

CHAPTER 33

[1]Martin Luther, quoted in *Money, Sex & Power* by Richard Foster (New York: Harper and Row, Publishers, 1985), p. 19.

[2]Leviticus 27:30,32.

[3]1 Corinthians 16:2.

[4]Acts 11:28,29.

[5]2 Corinthians 8:2,3.

[6]2 Corinthians 9:2.

[7]C. S. Lewis, *Mere Christianity* (New York: Macmillan, 1976), pp. 81,82.

CHAPTER 34

[1]Matthew 6:21.

[2]*Ibid.*

[3]*Ibid.*

[4]*Ibid.*

[5]*Ibid.*

[6]R. Kent Hughes, *Disciplines of a Godly Man* (Wheaton: Crossway Books, 1991), p. 177.

CHAPTER 35

[1]Mark 12:44.

[2]Philippians 4:15–17.

[3]Philippians 4:19.

[4]*Ibid.*

[5]Elizabeth O'Connor, "Letters to Scattered Pilgrims," quoted in *Disciplines for the Inner Life* by Bob Benson and Michael W. Benson (Waco: Word Books Publisher, 1985), p. 251.

CHAPTER 36

[1]Sue Monk Kidd, *God's Joyful Surprise* (San Francisco: Harper and Row, Publishers, 1987), p. 43.

[2]Paul Tournier, *Reflections on Life's Most Crucial Questions* (New York: Harper and Row, Publishers, 1976), p. 129.11.

CHAPTER 37

[1]Robert V. Thompson, *Unemployed* (Downers Grove: InterVarsity Press, 1983), p. 13.

[2]Luke 12:15.

[3]Luke 12:29–31.

[4]Paul Tournier, *Reflections on Life's Most Crucial Questions* (New York: Harper and Row, Publishers, 1976), p. 128.

CHAPTER 38

[1]Arthur Gordon, *A Touch of Wonder* (Old Tappan: Fleming H. Revell Company, 1984), p. 89.

[2]*Ibid.*

[3]Paul Tournier, *Reflections on Life's Most Crucial Questions* (New York: Harper and Row, Publishers, 1976), p. 170.

CHAPTER 39

[1]1 Corinthians 13:12 KJV.

[2]Paul Tournier, *Reflections on Life's Most Crucial Questions* (New York: Harper and Row, Publishers, 1976), p. 171.

CHAPTER 40

[1]H. Norman Wright, *Understanding the Man in Your Life* (Waco: Word Books Publisher, 1987), pp. 136,137.

[2]Jim Conway, *Men In Mid–Life Crisis* (Elgin: David C. Cook Publishing Company, 1978), flyleaf.

[3]H. Norman Wright, *Understanding the Man in Your Life* (Waco: Word Books Publisher, 1987), p. 139.

[4]*Ibid.*, p. 139.

[5]Proverbs 19:3.

[6]H. Norman Wright, *Understanding the Man in Your Life* (Waco: Word Books Publisher, 1987), p. 146.

CHAPTER 41

[1]H. Norman Wright, *Seasons of a Marriage* (Ventura: Regal Books, 1982), pp. 74,75.

[2]Romans 8:16–18.

[3]John Claypool, *Stages* (Waco: Word Books Publisher, 1977), pp. 68,69.

CHAPTER 42

[1]H. Norman Wright, *Seasons of a Marriage* (Ventura: Regal Books, 1982), p. 155.

CHAPTER 43

[1]Paul Tournier, *Reflections on Life's Most Crucial Questions* (New York: Harper and Row, Publishers, 1976), pp. 123,124.

[2]Acts 16:8–10.

[3]David Wilkerson, *I'm Not Mad At God* (Minneapolis: Bethany Fellowship, Inc., 1967), p. 32.

[4]Hannah Whitall Smith, *The Christian's Secret of a Happy Life* (Westwood: Fleming H. Revell Company, 1952), p. 101.

CHAPTER 44

[1]Hannah Whitall Smith, *The Christian's Secret of a Happy Life* (Westwood: Fleming H. Revell Company, 1952), p. 93.

CHAPTER 45

[1]2 Corinthians 6:14,15.

[2]Jeremiah 20:9.

[3]Keith Miller and Bruce Larson, *The Edge of Adventure* (Waco: Word Books Publisher, 1974), p. 214.

[4]Psalm 138:8.

[5]Gretchen Gaebelein Hull, "Frank Gaebelein: Character Before Career," *Christianity Today*, quoted in *Disciplines for the Inner Life* by Bob Benson and Michael W. Benson (Waco: Word Books Publisher, 1985), p. 91.

CHAPTER 46

[1]1 Kings 19:12 KJV.

[2]John Killinger, *The Centrality of Preaching in the Total Task of the Ministry* (Waco, Texas: Word Books Publisher, 1969), pp. 69.

[3]2 Corinthians 5:7 KJV.

[4]Hebrews 11:8.

[5]Paul Tournier, *Reflections on Life's Most Crucial Questions* (New York: Harper and Row, Publishers, 1976), p. 123.

[6]Hannah Whitall Smith, *The Christian's Secret of a Happy Life* (Westwood: Fleming H. Revell, 1952), p. 100.

CHAPTER 47

[1]William Temple, *Readings in St. John's Gospel* (London: The Macmillan Company, 1963), p. 24.

[2]Hebrews 4:15.

[3]*Ibid.*

[4]Luke 4:4.

[5]Luke 4:8.

[6]Luke 4:12.

[7]1 Corinthians 10:13.

[8]Oswald Chambers, *My Utmost for His Highest* (Westwood: Barbour and Company, Inc., Dodd Mead & Company, Inc., 1935), p. 79.

CHAPTER 48

[1]Matthew 5:29.

[2]Thomas a Kempis, *Imitation of Christ*, quoted in *Habitation of Dragons* by Keith Miller (Waco: Word Books Publishers, 1970), p. 110.

CHAPTER 49

[1]Mark 14:30.

[2]Mark 14:31.

[3]Luke 22:46.

[4]John 18:11.

[5]Mark 14:54.

[6]Luke 22:58–61.

[7]Luke 22:62.

[8]Thomas a Kempis, *The Imitation of Christ* (London: Collins, 1957), pp. 148,149.

CHAPTER 50

[1]1 Corinthians 10:12.

[2]Randy Alcorn, "Strategies To Keep From Falling," *Leadership*, Winter 1988, p. 47.

[3]Genesis 39:6–12.

[4]1 Timothy 6:11.

[5]1 John 2:1,2.

[6]Oswald Chambers, *My Utmost for His Highest* (Westwood: Barbour and Company, Inc., Dodd Mead & Company, Inc., 1935), p. 192.

CHAPTER 51

[1]Michel Quoist, *Prayers* (New York: Avon Books, A division of the Hearst Corporation, 1954), p. 1.

[2]Spencer Marsh, *God, Man, and Archie Bunker* (Tandem Productions, Inc., 1975). New York: Harper and Row Publishers, Inc.

³Quoted by Robert A. Raines in a sermon entitled "To See Each Other 'Real' Is Resurrection," in *The Splendor of Easter* edited by Floyd D. Thatcher (Waco: Word Books Publisher, 1972), pp. 23,24.

⁴Keith Miller and Bruce Larson, *The Edge of Adventure* (Waco: Word Books Publisher, 1974), p. 156.

CHAPTER 52

¹Matthew 18:12,13; Luke 15:3–7.

²Ezekiel 33:11 KJV.

³2 Timothy 2:13.

⁴Hebrews 13:8.

⁵Psalm 102:25–27.

⁶Richard D. Exley, *The Other God* (Plainfield: Logos International, 1979), p. 18.

CHAPTER 53

¹Genesis 18:10,12.

²Genesis 18:15.

³John Killinger, *For God's Sake, Be Human* (Waco: Word Books Publisher, 1970), p. 18.

⁴Bob Benson and Michael W. Benson, *Disciplines for the Inner Life* (Waco: Word Books Publisher, 1985), p. 256.

CHAPTER 54

¹Romans 5:6–8.

²A. W. Tozer, *The Knowledge of the Holy* (New York: Harper and Row Publishers, 1961), p. 97.

³1 John 4:18.

⁴Frederick B. Speakman, *The Salty Tang* (Westwood: Fleming H. Revell Company, 1954), p. 22.

CHAPTER 55

¹Keith Miller, *Habitation of Dragons* (Waco: Word Books Publisher, 1970), p. 123.

²J. S. Whale, *Christian Doctrine* (Cambridge: The University Press, 1956), pp. 145,146.

CHAPTER 56

¹Genesis 28:20,21.

²Quoted by John Killinger in *For God's Sake, Be Human* (Waco: Word Books Publisher, 1970), p. 47.

³Romans 8:29.

⁴Luke 15:19.

⁵Psalm 139:23.

⁶Philippians 3:10.

⁷A. W. Tozer, *The Knowledge of the Holy*, quoted in *Disciplines for the Inner Life* by Bob Benson and Michael W. Benson (Waco: Word Books Publisher, 1985), p. 3.

⁸Thomas R. Kelly, *A Testament of Devotion* (San Francisco: Harper and Row Publishers, 1941), p. 41.

CHAPTER 57

¹Henri J. Nouwen, *Gracias!*, quoted in *Disciplines for the Inner Life* by Bob Benson and Michael W. Benson (Waco: Word Books Publisher, 1985), p. 25.

²Betty Malz, *Prayers That Are Answered* (Lincoln: Chosen Books, 1980), p. 69.

³Isaiah 65:24.

⁴Matthew 6:10,11.

⁵J. Wallace Hamilton, *Where Now Is Thy God?* (Old Tappan: Fleming H. Revell Company, 1969), p. 47.

⁶Harry Emerson Fosdick, *The Meaning of Prayer* (New York: Association Press, 1962), p. 30.

CHAPTER 58

¹1 John 5:14.

²Francois Fenelon, quoted in *The Workbook of Living Prayer* by Maxie Dunnam (Nashville: The Upper Room, 1974), p. 35.

CHAPTER 59

¹Genesis 32:28.

²Genesis 32:26.

³James 5:16 KJV.

⁴Emilie Griffin, *Clinging — The Experience of Prayer*, quoted in *Disciplines for the Inner Life* by Bob Benson and Michael W. Benson (Waco: Word Books Publisher, 1985), pp. 232,233.

⁵Genesis 32:30.

⁶Pierre–Yves Emery, *Prayer at the Heart of Life* (Maryknoll: Orbis Books, 1975), pp. 136,137.

CHAPTER 60

¹Exodus 33:11.

²Psalm 42:7.

³Susan Annette Muto, *Pathways of Spiritual Living*, quoted in *Disciplines for the Inner Life* by Bob Benson and Michael W. Benson (Waco: Word Books Publisher, 1985), p. 49.

⁴Chaim Potok, *The Chosen*, 1967. (New York: The William Morris Agency, Inc.)

CHAPTER 61

[1]Abraham Joshua Heschel, *Man's Quest for God*, quoted in *Disciplines for the Inner Life* by Bob Benson and Michael W. Benson (Waco: Word Books Publisher, 1985), p. 6.

[2]Psalm 42:7.

[3]Genesis 32:30.

[4]John Baillie, *A Diary of Private Prayer*, quoted in *Disciplines for the Inner Life* by Bob Benson and Michael W. Benson (Waco: Word Books Publisher, 1985), p. 3.

[5]Alfred Lord Tennyson, quoted in *Where Now Is Thy God?* by J. Wallace Hamilton (Old Tappan: Fleming H. Revell Company, 1969), p. 14.

[6]Frederick Buechner, *The Magnificent Defeat* (New York: The Seabury Press, 1966), p. 23.

CHAPTER 62

[1]Henri J. Nouwen, *Gracias!*, quoted in *Disciplines for the Inner Life* by Bob Benson and Michael W. Benson (Waco: Word Books Publisher, 1985), p. 279.

[2]Ecclesiastes 1:14.

[3]Ecclesiastes 2:10,1.

[4]Ecclesiastes 2:4–6,8,11.

[5]Charles Hembree, *Pocket of Pebbles* (Grand Rapids: Baker Book House, 1969), p. 33.

[6]*An Anthology of George MacDonald* edited by C. S. Lewis, quoted in *Disciplines for the Inner Life* by Bob Benson and Michael W. Benson (Waco: Word Books Publisher, 1985), p. 311.

CHAPTER 63

[1]Norman Cousins, *Human Options*, quoted in *Disciplines for the Inner Life* by Bob Benson and Michael W. Benson (Waco: Word Books Publisher, 1985), p. 310.

[2]Maxie Dunnam, *Galatians, Ephesians, Philippians, Colossians, Philemon*, vol. 8, *The Communicator's Commentary* (Waco: Word Books Publisher, 1982), pp. 90,91.

CHAPTER 64

[1]Donald MacLeod, "Something Happened in Church," quoted in *The Twentieth–Century Pulpit*, edited by James W. Cox (Nashville: Abingdon, 1978), p. 134.

[2]Elizabeth O'Connor, *The Eighth Day of Creation*, quoted in *Disciplines for the Inner Life* by Bob Benson and Michael W. Benson (Waco: Word Books Publisher, 1985), p. 272.

CHAPTER 65

[1]James 1:27.

[2]St. Augustine, quoted in *Dawnings, Finding God's Light in the Darkness*, edited by Phyllis Hobe (New York: Guideposts Associates, Inc., 1981), p. 96.

BIBLIOGRAPHY

Alcorn, Randy. "Strategies To Keep From Falling," *Leadership*, Winter 1988, p. 47.

Benson, Bob, and Benson, Michael W. *Disciplines for the Inner Life*. Waco: Word Books Publisher, 1985.

Bisagno, John. *Positive Obedience*. Grand Rapids: Zondervan, 1979.

Buechner, Frederick. *The Magnificent Defeat*. New York: The Seabury Press, 1966.

Caloney, Joyce. "Confessions of a Happy Housewife." *Reader's Digest*, April 1982.

Campolo, Anthony. *Who Switched the Price Tags?* Waco: Word Books Publisher, 1986.

Chambers, Oswald. *My Utmost for His Highest*. Westwood: Barbour and Company, Inc., Dodd Mead & Company, Inc., 1935.

Claypool, John. *Stages*. Waco: Word Books Publisher, 1977.

Conway, Jim. *Men In Mid–Life Crisis*. Elgin: David C. Cook Publishing Company, 1978.

Cox, James W., ed. *The Twentieth-Century Pulpit*. Nashville: Abingdon, 1978.

Dobson, James. *Dr. Dobson Answers Your Questions*. Wheaton: Tyndale House Publishers, Inc., 1992.

Dobson, James C. *Straight Talk to Men and Their Wives*. Waco: Word Books Publisher, 1980.

Donaldson, Hal, and Dobson, Kenneth M., eds. *Pleasing God, Pleasing You*. Visalia: Onward Books, 1992.

Dunnam, Maxie. *Galatians, Ephesians, Philippians, Colossians, Philemon*. Vol. 8. *The Communicator's Commentary* . Waco: Word Books Publisher, 1982.

Dunnam, Maxie. *The Workbook of Living Prayer*. Nashville: The Upper Room, 1974.

Emery, Pierre–Eves. *Prayer at the Heart of Life*. Maryknoll: Orbis Books, 1975.

Exley, Richard. *Blue–Collar Christianity*. Tulsa: Honor Books, 1989.

Exley, Richard. *Building Relationships That Last: Life's Bottom Line*. Tulsa: Honor Books, 1990.

Exley, Richard. *Perils of Power*. Tulsa: Honor Books, 1988.

Exley, Richard. *The Other God*. Plainfield: Logos International, 1979.

Exley, Richard. *The Rhythm of Life*. Tulsa: Honor Books, 1987.

Fosdick, Harry Emerson. *The Meaning of Prayer*. New York: Association Press, 1962.

Foster, Richard. *Money, Sex & Power*. New York: Harper and Row, Publishers, 1985.

Foster, Richard. *The Freedom of Simplicity*. San Francisco: Harper and Row, Publishers, 1981.

Gordon, Arthur. *A Touch of Wonder*. Old Tappan: Fleming H. Revell Company, 1984.

Hamilton, J. Wallace. *Where Now Is Thy God?* Old Tappan: Fleming H. Revell Company, 1969.

Hembree, Charles. *Pocket of Pebbles*. Grand Rapids: Baker Book House, 1969.

Hobe, Phyllis, ed. *Dawnings, Finding God's Light in the Darkness*. New York: Guideposts Associates, Inc., 1981.

Hobe, Phyllis, ed. *Tapestries of Life*. Philadelphia: A. J. Holman Company, 1974.

Houston, James. *The Transforming Friendship*. Batavia: Lion Publishing Corporation, 1989.

Hughes, R. Kent. *Disciplines of a Godly Man*. Wheaton: Crossway Books, 1991.

Humes, James. *Churchill: Speaker of the Century*. Briarcliff Manor, New York: Stein and Day Publishers, Scarborough House, 1980.

Kelly, Thomas R. *A Testament of Devotion*. San Francisco: Harper and Row, Publishers, 1941.

Kidd, Sue Monk. *God's Joyful Surprise*. San Francisco: Harper and Row, Publishers, 1987.

Killinger, John. *For God's Sake, Be Human*. Waco: Word Books Publisher, 1970.

Killinger, John. *The Centrality of Preaching in the Total Task of the Ministry*. Waco, Texas: Word Books Publisher, 1969.

Kushner, Harold. *When All You've Ever Wanted Isn't Enough*. New York: Summit Books, A Division of Simon and Schuster, Inc., 1986.

Larson, Bruce. *The Relational Revolution*. Waco: Word Books Publisher, 1976.

Lewis, C. S. *Mere Christianity*. New York: Macmillan, 1976.

Ludwig, Charles. *He Freed Britain's Slaves*. Scottdale: Herald Press, 1977.

MacDonald, Gordon. *Rebuilding Your Broken World*. Nashville: Oliver Nelson, A Division of Thomas Nelson Publishers, 1988.

Malz, Betty. *Prayers That Are Answered*. Lincoln: Chosen Books, 1980.

Marsh, Spencer. *God, Man, and Archie Bunker*. Tandem Productions, Inc., 1975. New York: Harper and Row, Publishers, Inc.

Mayhall, Jack, and Mayhall, Carole. *Marriage Takes More Than Love*. Colorado Springs: Navpress, 1978.

Miller, Keith. *Habitation of Dragons*. Waco: Word Books Publisher, 1970.

Miller, Keith, and Larson, Bruce. *The Edge of Adventure*. Waco: Word Books Publisher, 1974.

Morris, Desmond. *Intimate Behavior*. New York: Random House, 1971.

Muck, Terry C. "From the Editor." *Leadership*, Fall 1984.

Osborne, Cecil G. *The Art of Becoming a Whole Person*. Waco: Word Books Publisher, 1978.

Patterson, Ben. *The Grand Essentials*. Waco: Word Books Publisher, 1987.

Potok, Chaim. *The Chosen*, 1967. New York: The William Morris Agency, Inc.

Quoist, Michel. *Prayers*. New York: Avon Books, A Division of the Hearst Corporation, 1954.

Robbins, Paul D. "Must Men Be Friendless?" *Leadership*, Fall 1984.

Samuel, Dorothy T. *Fun and Games in Marriage*. Waco: Word Books Publisher, 1973.

Shibley, David. *Heavenly Incentives For Earthly Living*. Old Tappan: Fleming H. Revell Company, Chosen Books, 1988.

Smith, Hannah Whitall. *The Christian's Secret of a Happy Life*. Westwood: Fleming H. Revell, 1952.

Speakman, Frederick B. *The Salty Tang*. Westwood: Fleming H. Revell Company, 1954.

Tan, Paul Lee. *Encyclopedia of 7,700 Illustrations: Signs of the Times*. Chicago: Assurance Publishers, 1979.

Temple, Williams. *Readings in St. John's Gospel*. London: The Macmillan Company, 1963.

Thatcher, Floyd D., ed. *The Splendor of Easter*. Waco: Word Books Publisher, 1972.

Thomas a Kempis. *The Imitation of Christ*. London: Collins, 1957.

Thompson, Robert V. *Unemployed*. Downers Grove: InterVarsity Press, 1983.

Tournier, Paul. *Reflections on Life's Most Crucial Questions*. New York: Harper and Row, Publishers, 1976.

Tozer, A. W. *The Knowledge of the Holy*. New York: Harper and Row, Publishers, 1961.

Tozer, A. W. *The Pursuit of God*. Harrisburg: Christian Publications, Inc., 1948.

Whale, J. C. *Christian Doctrine*. Cambridge: The University Press, 1956.

Wilkerson, David. *I'm Not Mad At God*. Minneapolis: Bethany Fellowship, Inc., 1967.

Wright, H. Norman. *Communication: Key to Your Marriage*. Ventura: Regal Books, 1974.

Wright, H. Norman. *Seasons of a Marriage*. Ventura: Regal Books, 1982.

Wright, H. Norman. *Understanding the Man in Your Life*. Waco: Word Books Publisher, 1987.